A
Christian
Family
in Action

A Christian Family in Action

MIKE PHILLIPS

Bethany Fellowship INC.
MINNEAPOLIS, MINNESOTA 55438

Copyright © 1977
Bethany Fellowship, Inc.
All rights reserved

Published by Bethany Fellowship, Inc.
6820 Auto Club Road, Minneapolis, Minnesota 55438

Printed in the United States of America

Library of Congress Cataloging in Publication Data:

Phillips, Mike, 1946-
    A Christian family in action.

    Includes bibliographical references.
    1. Family—Religious life.   I. Title.
BV4526.2.P47   248'.4   77-1887
ISBN 0-87123-085-2

To our parents

who raised us, not perfectly but
wisely, and who are in large measure
responsible for any godly thing
we can pass along to our own children;

To our brothers and sisters,

Cathy, Janet, Diana, Jim, Doug,
who were the framework of the
families in which we grew and
learned so much; and

To Rolf,

a special friend, and a
special man of God.

MIKE PHILLIPS was raised in California, graduated from Humboldt University, and had every intention of pursuing a career in physics or math. But, instead, he got hooked on books. Beginning with a small, part-time selling effort in an upstairs apartment, he branched out in earnest and now heads *ONE WAY, LTD.,* and two of the largest Christian bookstores in northern California.

He and Judy were married in 1971, and have two sons, Patrick and Robin. Judy does all the accounting for the stores and "handles" the active children. Home is Eureka, California, and the great adventures of Mike's life are his family and the delights of the bookstore ministry.

Foreword

I have sometimes been appalled at the way some people have put my own teaching on family life into practice. What we have experienced as a helpful, indeed a liberating, structure for family life has been turned into a system of rigid rules. The saving grace of Spirit-directed application has somehow been missed.

What I like about this book is the healthy balance between biblical principle and Spirit-given common sense. Especially so since it came out of personal struggle. That gives it a stamp of authenticity.

The story line grips you. The author takes you into the intimacy of his own family. You share with Mike and Judy Phillips some of the difficulties and frustrations, the joys and victories, of trying to put biblical principles for family living into practice. You don't only hear about Christian family life, you see it happen. And you know it's for real.

You come away from your visit in their family with a new appreciation for the personal ministry of the Holy Spirit. He meets each one of us right where we are. He orders our families according to the biblical pattern, but in ways that are infinitely varied. The important thing is to remain open and flexible so He can work with us.

Larry Christenson

Preface

This is the story of our family discovering how to make God's principles work in our lives. We are a young family; therefore this is but the first chapter of God's dealing with us. We have had but a bare glimpse of many of these truths. As my wife and I have groped and struggled, as does every other young couple, we have realized some fundamental things about how a family operates under biblical principles.

We have discovered that God's structure for the family is based on three relationships: the authority of Jesus over the husband, the authority of the husband over the wife, and the authority of the parents over the children. Three words describe these three relationships: commitment, love, and discipline. When these words become alive and begin to operate in the daily lives of people, God builds a family.

This is the story of the beginning of that process in our lives. I am not a great scholar. I do not have years of experience in marriage counseling, child psychology, or family guidance. I am a businessman and my wife is a homemaker. The only credentials we have to offer are several years of being taught by the Lord in things relating to our daily struggles. Though not an in-depth study, neither has it been written somewhere far removed from practical living. This book has risen out of our daily experiences as we have sought to follow the Lord in what we do.

And I think this is a valuable perspective and will be an encouragement to others facing similiar questions. After all, the body of Christ is nothing more than ordinary people like you and me doing our best to follow the Lord in what He gives us to do each day. We offer this book to you in that light. It is our prayer that through these experiences, both failures and triumphs, you will discover ways to implement God's love and authority into your family.

Mike Phillips
Eureka, California

Acknowledgments

In His molding of our lives, God never works in a vacuum. He uses people and situations to show us His character and to work His attributes into us. Judy and I have always been keenly aware of the impact many people have had on our spiritual growth and development. So in thinking about whom to acknowledge as having been influential in the development of this book, the many, many people we love who have ministered in various ways to us naturally came to our minds. And it is these special people we would like to thank. Of course it is impossible to name personally everyone who has been used of God in our lives. But they know who they are and to them we simply say, "Thank you for touching us."

But we would like specifically to mention a few who stand out, not only as dear to us but as ones whose lives have definitely brought us closer to God in unforgettable ways. We think of Bill Frazee, a dear friend who, along with Joanne T., was one of my first critics and editors. And then there are Jim and Joanne, Mike and Marianne, Charles and Janice, the Ellises, George, Clarry, Rey, Larry L., Sam and Lou, Bill Treguboff, Richard and Phyllis. For them and all the others whose lives are deeply woven into our growth, we thank God for the blessing they have been.

Then there are the innumerable people whose prayer, support, and interest have contributed to the ministry of our store and all that it is becoming. God bless you. Many we do not even know personally, yet they have greatly contributed to a ministry of God. But how could we not mention Rosemarie, Laurene, Carolyn, Amos, Wilma, Barbara, Marybeth, Martha, David, as well as Joyce and our faithful Maxine, whose help at the store during this part of our lives was crucial. And of course there is Mary, without whom, in several ways, this book could never have been written.

CONTENTS

COMMITMENT

Commit your way to the Lord; trust in him, and he will act.—Ps. 37:5 (RSV)

Wives, submit to your husbands as you do to the Lord. For the husband is the wife's authority in the same way that Christ is the head of His own Body the church. So as the church is subject to Christ, let women also be subject to their husbands in everything they do.

Husbands, love your wives in the same way that Jesus loved the church and gave His life for it, to cleanse, purify, and perfect it.—Eph. 5:22-26 (author's paraphrase)

Spiritual authority is rooted in the sacrifice of one's self... it is a paradox. Jesus said, "If any one would be first he must be last of all, and servant of all." [1]

There is a twofold aspect to commitment: to God and to one another. The foundation of all relationships and growth is commitment to the Lord and submission to His authority. Once this foundation has been laid, commitment to one another takes on equal importance. Especially in marriage, the commitment of husband and wife to each other must be a more basic ingredient even than their love.

The relationship which binds a man and woman together is a relationship of love which is practiced on the level of a daily commitment to one another. God has designed this love to function through the authority He has placed in the family. This is no worldly authority. It is an authority based on sacrifice. If love is to blossom and mature, both husband and wife must commit themselves to the functioning of this authority. The wife must lay down her life and submit to her husband. The husband must sacrifice himself, lay down his life for his wife. This is how authority works and how love grows. There is no other way.

1

Changing Priorities

"Mrs. Phillips, this is Dr. Martin's office. The doctor would like some more tests. Could you go to the lab immediately?"

"Yes. I'll arrange for a substitute for my class and be right over. Why? What's the matter?" asked Judy.

"The doctor suspects that yours may not be a true pregnancy.... But don't worry. The daughter of one of the nurses here had the same thing and she was able to have children later," answered the nurse on the phone.

After quickly making the necessary arrangements, Judy left for Eureka. Although trying to remain calm, the natural fears and anxieties which plague a pregnancy began to press in upon her. She stopped first at the bookstore. The quaver in her voice as she told me of the confusing phone call told me she was close to tears. We tried to be matter of fact. But we were both shaken.

Not many minutes after Judy had gone on to the lab the phone rang for me. I heard a voice say, "This is Jack Martin. I thought I'd better fill you in on what's happening so that you and Judy won't be too upset. Here is the thing. By this time, Judy's increase in size should have been about the size of a grapefruit, which it obviously isn't."

As he talked my mind drifted back. We had been watching her weight so carefully. When the scales showed five-pound jumps on two consecutive days, we took immediate notice. At the same time there was an increasingly more "pregnant" look, also peculiar at this early stage. Up to that point, Judy had seen the doctor only once. When the Tuesday for her next scheduled appointment came, the doctor also noted the rapid rise in weight and ordered a urine test for that same day. "Simply a routine check," he assured us. It was not until Thursday of that week, when the doctor called me at the store, that we heard the results of that test.

"That was the reason for the urine test last Tuesday," the doctor continued, "just to see if there might be something unusual going on. And the results do seem to indicate an abnormality of some kind. At this point it looks as if Judy could have what is sometimes called a false pregnancy, or a 'mole.' Of course, it is too soon to be sure. So we are doing another test today. But in case it does turn out to be a mole, I have scheduled surgery for next week. BUT DON'T WORRY . . . moles used to be a little dangerous, but nowadays they are rarely malignant and can easily be removed. . . ."

As I put down the receiver my reaction was much like Judy's for the rest of the day—blank. It was impossible to really think about what was happening; it was coming so fast. Especially when it was so closely linked in time to our friend's daughter Angela's death and to Carol's miscarriage. It seemed more like the hand of fate than the hand of the Lord.

* * *

Growing into adulthood from adolescense is demanding enough. But to stick a marriage in the middle of the process insures dramatic (and usually painful) change. I had scarcely begun to get the hang of living on my own when I found myself suddenly coping with the adjustments of living with a wife. The first months were wonderful. We loved one another tremendously and wore "all-day smiles." The comments from our friends such as, "you'll see," and "just you wait," warned us of the bumpy water ahead, but we took virtually no notice.

As I look back now to our very first meeting, I see both a misunderstanding which developed and a bond which formed. These two factors contributed to this blithe lack of foresight we exhibited. One would cause a rift to develop between us, but the other would provide the healing to make us one.

Judy and I met through shared Christian activities at school. Her musical abilities were the first thing to catch my eye. I noticed her playing her guitar and singing at many of our campus meetings. Before long we began to go to church together. Then we somehow became involved in the Sunday school of a small and struggling church several miles from town. Later we began weekly Bible study and prayer times with a group of junior high students and saw God work many exciting things. There was a common commitment which grew deep and strong between us—a shared vision. We prayed together, studied together, talked together about our problems, our growth, our joys.

There was no hint of romance. We were simply two very close friends sharing a deep spiritual bond because of all we were involved in together. God was at work in our lives in thrilling ways and it was exciting to share it.

Our Christian bookstore began during this time also and we were both a part of it from the beginning, another common interest and shared goal. We attended Inter-Varsity's Urbana Convention together, and God lit a fire under us to expand the store and move out mightily in faith! It seemed that in everything which touched our lives as individuals, Judy and I shared it together.

There was, however, a misunderstanding developing. Though it was not apparent to us at the time, our relationship was almost entirely centered around activities. So as we grew closer and began to talk of marriage, and then later when we were married, all along I conceived of our relationship as one of ministering to others in Christian service. That's how it began, and somehow in my mind that's where it would remain.

So though the activities were perhaps an unsuitable basis for our relationship, they did create a very special bond between us. We were involved in what to us was a high calling of God. Though for many months there was no romantic connection at all, Judy and I were unmistakably best friends. We really were best friends in every way. We really liked each other. It was very special.

But one day stands out in my memory. Several of us went to the beach after church. It was a grey day, nothing much to do. We were sitting around quietly and Judy picked up her guitar and very softly sang,

> He walks in the rain by my side,
> I'll cling to the warmth of His gentle hand.
> The leaves will bow down when He walks by,
> And morning bells will chime . . . .

It was soft and beautiful. I'd never quite heard that something in her voice before. I knew she was singing about Jesus. But somehow I think I knew she singing to me too.

The rest of that day there just seemed to be a great bond between us—of caring, of comraderie. We said little. We didn't have to. It was just there. I think I began to sense on that day that Judy might be my wife.

As the months passed we gradually found ourselves growing more traditionally "attached" to one another. And then there was that memorable night in the balcony of our church when I told Judy I thought she was to be my wife. She was really taken by surprise. I hadn't even held her hand until we'd been seeing each other almost daily for ten months. And now this. What a shock!

And still these two forces were growing deeper and stronger—my desire for us to minister as a team, and the deep bond of our friendship.

When our wedding day came, our love for each other was so deep and our excitement so great over what God had in store for the future that we knew our marriage was going to be something marvelous! We asked our pastor to open the wedding ceremony with a ten-minute talk on commitment, how our marriage would revolve around our commitment and service to Jesus. We wanted everyone to know we were joining as a "team" to serve the Lord. We idealized our blissful life together and unknowingly stumbled forward.

We laugh now looking back over some of the letters we wrote prior to our marriage:

> The future is so bright. . . .
> Our relationship is so much greater. . . .
> It'll be so neat I can't believe it. . . .
>
> —Mike
>
> We are looking peacefully and realistically to the future.
> We will be starting out miles ahead of so many couples.
> I don't understand how we can understand each other
> so deeply.
>
> —Judy

Yes, Judy and I faced unexpected change, and it did not take long. Our most severe obstacle turned out to be one that sounded so "simple"—dying to ourselves. Jesus assured us over and over that only in doing so will we discover any lasting meaning in our relationships. It is a simple concept of putting the other person first. But how we do struggle!

Perhaps a newly married couple cannot adequately prepare for what faces them. I know the struggles and failings in a marriage are used to make the relationship strong and deep. Through the falling-and-getting-back-up-again process God builds strength. Judy and I were fortunate. Had the Lord not preserved our love for each other, we have often wondered what the result might have been. Adjustments must be made and a marriage thrives or dies according to how it copes with change.

Judy entered our marriage with a serious future in several areas, either as a harpist, as a school teacher, or working in our bookstore. Because of her abilities she continued to pursue all these areas, even though the time and commitment required often caused problems. Neither of us realized that we hadn't considered the effect her involvement in these activities would have on our marriage relationship. God had given Judy some obvious skills and we just naturally assumed they were to be followed. We as yet had no inkling that the creativity God puts within a woman must be surrendered to her husband and their marriage for its fruitfulness to be realized.

Many of Judy's interests therefore slowly began to be more independent of our marriage and contributed less and less to it. Being completely unaware of the principle involved here, I failed to provide any decisive leadership in her activities. I was at the same time involved in *my* interests and failed to see the conflict and imbalance growing in our marriage. My shortsightedness concerning this aspect of our marriage was clearly evidenced by a letter I wrote Judy two months before our wedding: "You will have your path and I will have mine. . . . We can't be bound to each other. . . . Love has got to be free. . . . "

So Judy brought into our marriage her potential career as a promising harpist and school teacher, fully expecting to pursue both goals as before. I brought into our marriage all my expectations for Judy as a Christian worker to contribute and to share in my goals for service and outreach. I envisioned our marriage as an exciting road to Christian ministry—the expanding opportunities of our Christian bookstore, Bible studies with young people, church work, and the like. A team, that's what we were.

We had never thoroughly discussed how my goals for our marriage and Judy's goals fit together. We both simply assumed our lives would continue on as before. Only now we would be together. Other than that nothing much would change. I had a very democratic outlook on marriage. I saw no particular need for a leader. God would lead. Judy's teaching, our ministry with young people,

Judy's harp career, my vision for the continued expansion of the store—though vastly different, these things would all somehow fit together because God had brought us together. My thoughts went no further than that. The deepening growth of a marriage relationship was something to which I had given little consideration. For me marriage was like a partnership, a corporation. We were to be accomplishing a job. That's why God had brought us together—to minister, to serve, to reach out.

Before long the tension began to be felt. My "ministry" with people took on many forms. There were activities with young people several nights a week, lengthy counseling phone calls two or three evenings a week, and a full daytime schedule of school teaching in the morning and working in the store afternoons. In addition to this there were several young men who lived with us in our small two-bedroom house at one time or another through most of our first married year.

Judy, too, carried a full schedule. She handled the store in the morning, attended school in the afternoon, and came home to an evening of being both wife to me and "mother" to our houseguest of the moment. Unknowingly I was forcing Judy to conform to my concept of serving others. I assumed she shared my idealistic view of Christian ministry.

She felt the strain of my expectations, complicated by her independent pursuit of her own goals. She was not unsympathetic to my view of marriage, but serving others was only one aspect of it for her. There was also her credential work and future teaching, as well as her harp studies, to be considered.

The first tensions between us were small, almost unnoticeable. We chalked it up to "marital adjustments." "Just getting used to each other," we would say. But we were heading in different directions. Though joined together, we were operating separately.

Our time alone was rare. Evenings were spent either at some church function, or with me on the phone or

in the company of our particular boarder of the moment.
I was unknowingly forcing Judy to conform to my image
of a "spiritual life" and was overlooking the personal
creativity trying to blossom from within her. Not only
this, I also had not the slightest notion that she had deep
and real needs as a woman. I had said, "I will love you
and cherish you," but was doing just the opposite. I was
operating as if witnessing, counseling, praying, and other
spiritual activities—i.e., "ministry" as I saw it—could
satisfy the deepest longings of a wife to be loved by her
husband. The conflict grew and intensified slowly.

After a year, it was unmistakable.

We were having problems!

Regular debates complete with tears, questions, and
aching hearts became part of our established routine.

"Why can't you smile at dinner?" I would begin.

"Why can't we just once have dinner alone?" Judy
would retort. "Is that asking too much?"

"We do sometimes," I would answer defensively.

"I know . . . "

"God gave us this opportunity," I would hastily in-
terrupt. "We can't ignore it. Dave has problems and it's
up to us to minister to him. You always have a cloud
about you whenever he's around. How can you love him
if you don't even smile?"

"But why are *we* always the ones to help?" Judy
would continue.

"Who else is there? Where could Dave go if we didn't
take him in?"

"Plenty of places!" Judy would fire back.

"It's just for a while," I would reassure her.

"It's always 'just for a while,' " she would insist.
"When he's gone it'll be someone else. When are we going
to live like ordinary people!"

So it went. We groped and struggled for answers, often
taking out our frustrations on each other. I pressured
Judy to be unselfish, to "love" these people we were

involved with. Judy's spirit balked, knowing that they were taking me away from her. The horrible days when I would walk to the store in a cloud of gloom, leaving Judy sobbing behind at home, were all too many. We didn't know what was happening to us. As yet we still had no idea that we each had to lay down many of our preconceived ideas and attitudes.

So on we went, probing every possibility for a speck of common ground which might exist amid the array of our scattered activities and goals. We longed for the harmony we had once known together. But it just wasn't there. The struggle continued.

*   *   *

Some time during our second year of marriage, God slowly began to reveal to me some direction. Through several books I was reading, I began to glimpse something of my proper role in our marriage. The single word *authority* was for me the touchstone, the turning point. I had been guilty of two errors. The first, due to a lack of understanding, was in my thinking that marriage in all of its aspects was somehow to be equal. Both my reticent personality and my training contributed to this idea. Secondly, in sheer self-centeredness I had viewed our marriage as entirely built about *my* plans, *my* walk with the Lord, *my* service—*my* everything. I had given little consideration to the struggles Judy had undoubtedly been experiencing in trying to adapt herself to life with me.

The Christian Family by Larry Christenson was particularly helpful in scripturally demonstrating to me that in a godly marriage the husband and wife do not occupy identical or equal roles. They are equal in importance, yes, but not in function. Authority was the key. God ordained marriage in such a way that the man was designated to be the leader, the ruler, the decision-maker. The role of the woman was not an inferior role, simply a different one. The man was to be the "authority," and the woman was to be the responder to that authority. The man's headship over his wife, far from stifling her personality, ministers to her and provides the best possible atmosphere for her individuality to flow out and express itself. Christenson says, "Upon man is laid the authority to rule. But with it comes heavy care and hard labor. . . . " I agreed as I read further, "Gladly would the man allow the rule to pass out of his hands—if at the same time he were released from the care and responsibility." [2]

"I do not want to rule," I thought. "Authority may be natural to some men, but not to me."

But there did not appear to be an easy way out. There did not appear to be *any* way out! The Bible is clear, "Husbands, love your wives as Christ loved the church." Jesus not only died for the church, He loved the church, He sacrificed himself daily for the church, and yet He is the head of the church—its leader, its ruler, its authority.

And in our marriage that apparently was to be my role towards Judy.

This signified tremendous adjustment for me! It began a whole new struggle. "Okay. If my job is to be an authority in my home, I'll do it," I consented. "But what does it mean? How do you go about *being* a godly ruler, authority, head, in a daily way?"

I pestered the Lord with questions as I continued my reading.

> [Husbands]—you must aspire to nothing less in your relationship to your wife. You must emulate Him [Jesus] in all your ways. . . . When you fail, you not only fail your wife, you also fail to represent your Lord's love for His church. . . . On both husband and wife God laid His commandments; there is no less stringency in one instance than in the other. . . . Christ's authority in the home . . . is centered in the husband. . . . It is his responsibility to see that it is exercised, and exercised properly in ways that honor Christ.[3]

[Men] are heads over [their] wives ... it is a headship in love that is oriented toward doing all that one can for his wife ... headship means love; that is giving oneself.[4]

All authority is from God, but it is given for the good of those under it ... the character of authority has changed [through Christ]. ... Now authority becomes a service, and subjection is submission to being served. No one may clothe himself with authority. But whoever has received authority from God must hold it firmly. He must have faith in it and must maintain it, out of faithfulness to God, not for selfish reasons. ... God's authority often comes into our life through human authority.[5]

Out of my study of authority emerged two aspects I knew had been missing in our marriage and which I saw as the key to my loving Judy as I should. First I saw that with Jesus as my example, I must lay down my life for Judy. As her authority I must be her servant. Secondly, I saw that as her authority God had set me over her to rule her, to guide her, to lead her.

Mine was a twofold and paradoxical responsibility— to be an authority over her by serving her and giving my life for her. This was confirmed by my pastor in a counseling session I had with him concerning our problems. "Make her number one," he told me emphatically. "Spare nothing. Love her. Give yourself to her completely, even if it means laying down your other interests and activities. She has got to be your main concern."

By now it was clear that the initial responsibility for amending the situation lay with me. If I was to be the leader, the first item of business certainly had to be getting our marriage back on the track. A determination set in to conquer our problems whatever it took. I continued to search for practical answers, looking for things I could change which would help. I wanted very much to follow my pastor's advice, but I still wasn't sure how.

The Lord then began to show me slowly that my life could not be measured by my "service" to Him through activities. No, the only true measure must be following the example of Jesus and the church. And that meant my giving myself utterly to this woman who was my wife. I had had it all backwards. I had seen her coming to join *me* so that *we* could serve the Lord *together*. By emphasizing the "we" in my mind, I mistakenly thought we were "one" as the Lord intended. But I now began to see that our unity, our oneness, could never stem from what we *did* together, but *must come from the relationship we had between one another*. I saw that my life, my career, my service, my activity meant *nothing* alongside my giving my life for this woman I loved. I had virtually done nothing to give my life for her. I had never tried to really understand her, to love her innermost being. We had done many things together, and in a sense we were a "team," but we had yet to discover that bond of unity and love which grows out of a commitment—a commitment to lay yourself down to meet the other's deepest need.

These were painful realizations for me. I knew there were many things I was going to have to lay down, to give up. One by one I saw that many of my activities and involvements were going to have to be eliminated. This was not easy. I agonized over the attempt to disentangle myself.

I keenly remember one night when a close friend was forced to move out of his apartment and had no place to go. We discussed it. Judy said she was willing to have him live with us "for a while." Though it tore me apart, I knew I must say no to him at this time even though it meant he had to sleep in his van instead. I had to make a conscious decision, "Our time to minister will come again. But right now I've got to put my wife first, no matter what the consequences."

It may sound cruel. But we earlier had tried to minister whenever an opportunity came along and it had driven us far apart. I now knew that learning to say "no" was a big part of the answer.

My relationship with our young people also began to change. This too was terribly difficult. They had been a part of my life deeply for several years, and I wanted to hold onto them. But somehow the Lord loosened my grasp and kept my eyes firmly on the goal. I had to constantly reaffirm my decision to put the Lord's solution above my own immediate desires. Saying "no" continued to be extremely difficult for a long time, especially when I was constantly plagued by the thought, "I am failing them. What will they do without my help?" But the way remained clear and after some months I became accustomed to the idea that there were other Christians in the world. It didn't all depend on me. The Lord could take care of these people and situations well enough without my help. My wife was my concern, not hundreds of other people.

Over the next year we gradually made some headway against our endless string of activities. It was easy to think the hectic pace was merely temporary and would resolve itself in time. "Once the store settles down a little ... as soon as we get the house fixed up ... when our marriage is flowing a little more smoothly ... THEN ... "—so why try to change it now. But the "slower day a comin' " is pure illusion. Temporary pressures last forever unless they are dealt with. So we consciously made ourselves say "no," turning our backs on many worthwhile activities. We were firm in our resolve to slow the pace and cut down five and six nights a week to one or two. We had to put our time spent quietly together at the top of the priority list.

Our church involvement was also affected. As my priorities began to change, I saw the need to set aside at least one day a week to spend at home with Judy. Since our bookstore was open six days a week, that day had to be Sunday. And if Sunday was the only day available, then Sunday would be the at-home-day. In carrying out this resolve to put Judy first I encountered considerable opposition, because our participation in church activities was affected. Now and then we even found it necessary not to attend church at all on a certain day. But that did not cause me to abandon the plan. I saw the wisdom of a weekly "Sabbath" day of rest and was determined it should be a part of our schedule—whether or not it occasionally interfered with church attendance.

This all caused tremendous change in me. For the first time, I think, I was becoming a "married man." Though our problems were far from solved, that special bond we had known all along rose again to affirm itself. The once-fading embers began to glow more brightly. I began to really enjoy being at home with my wife more than anything else. It had taken some time and a decided effort, but all my activities and "being on the go for the Lord" ceased to attract me. The changes were going deep. Life began to center more and more around my wife and home and family. No longer was an exalted (and unrealistic) vision of "Christian Service" what I wanted to do. I simply wanted to quietly live the life that Jesus taught by giving myself wholeheartedly to my wife and family. Whatever else the Lord led me into beyond that would be His concern, not mine.

I knew that ministry to others would be a part of our life together later, but only as we practically learned to love each other now. And what gave me great confidence through these changes was knowing that they were coming from God himself. My initial efforts to obey the counsel I had received from books and other Christians had been feeble, yet sincere. But once I made those attempts the Lord took over and altered my whole value structure. My new priorities became quite natural to me. The Lord knew my deepest needs and was bringing me to the point where He could minister to them most effectively.

At the same time God was showing me further truths about my role as the authority in our marriage. He began to reveal to me some ways I could love Judy as He intended. There were two encircling "arms" to this God-given authority. My headship over her and love for her worked out this way: I must lead her and serve her. And I began to become aware of some personal needs which Judy shared in common with all women—the need for affection and love. I also saw the tremendous effort she was making to live the life of Jesus. She needed help and support, not my constant criticism. It had become easy for me to take Judy for granted because of her maturity and spiritual commitment. But at this point, Judy needed encouragement and support. These needs could never be met by meetings and activities and throngs of people. Judy didn't need anything but me right then— ALL of me. This was how I had to serve her—with my time, my interest, my encouragement.

But at the same time I had to lead her. God began to show me some things Judy had to lay down. I was struggling to lay down many of my earlier preconceptions of our marriage, and now I saw that Judy, too, had incorrect preconceptions which had to go. I saw that her career plans were not contributing to our marriage. In fact, like many of my "activities," they were doing it harm. Just as it was clear that I had not been serving her, it was clear that she had been largely independent of me.

* * *

In trying to convey these things, I tried to have authority without being authoritarian. My role as a successful "head" of the family was to be far more managerial than dictatorial. If a problem existed, then it was my responsibility to correct it. And a problem certainly existed within both of us. "Early Mosaic law made it clear that the emotional well-being of a wife is the specific responsibility of her husband." [6] The tears I left in Judy's eyes so many mornings were clear evidence that she needed some emotional cheering up. So I would do my part (back off, stop criticizing, and stop forcing her to be someone she wasn't), and I would lead her in doing her part (submit to me and my life). No matter how softly I tried to walk and no matter how gently I tried to peddle it, when it came down to the bottom line, it was stark and bare, "You must give up your career plans and throw in with me—submit to my goals, my aspirations, and my career."

I admit it sounds peculiar for me to have said that to Judy when I was going through the same struggle to give up things. But that is how it came about. I did not have my own house completely in order before I began to guide Judy in getting hers cleaned up. We each had one simple charge laid before us—to willingly lay down the expectations we had brought into our marriage and totally recommit our lives to each other. For me that meant assuming my proper role as the head and authority in the family, serving the family. For Judy it meant submitting to that leading and that authority. For me it meant withdrawing from activities and involvements so I could spend time with Judy. For Judy it meant laying aside her career plans so she could be totally my wife. Neither option was easy. The "laying down" process was painful, and we both resisted often.

Marriage is not the fifty-fifty proposition it is so often said to be. Instead, both husband and wife *must* go all the way, giving 100 percent if it is to work. We were discovering that. We both had to pull out all the stops, lay aside *every* preconceived plan and hope we had, and die to everything we cared about which didn't relate specifically to our relationship.

So I asked Judy to quit school and withdraw from the orchestra. At the same time I continued to withdraw from my involvements.

For my part, it is summed up by C. S. Lewis in his tape series, *The Four Loves.* The love a man must have for a woman is so complete, so total, so inexhaustible, yet so practical, that no sacrifice is too great for her. This love of a man for his wife is "like the king who after twenty years of marriage still hopes the beggar woman he married will one day learn to wash behind her ears."

The words stopped me cold.

"Do I love Judy anything like that?" I asked myself. I had to admit I didn't. We had been married barely two years and already I had grown critical and cold. I had married a queen, yet treated her with less patience and respect than this king did his beggar wife. I had much to learn in the area of devotion and sacrifice. Though it didn't become easy overnight, it did become clear.

For us both it remained very difficult to release from our grasp our desire for fairness. The idea that "everything has to be equal" dies hard. If the Lord required me to lay down something, then deep inside a part of me was watching to make certain Judy also had to go through an equal share of the process. Neither of us wanted to be the one to go all out. There was that slight element of holding back. It is a natural human tendency. Our egos, our selves, were fighting to retain a foothold.

But even as this struggle went on, we both had been reading *The Christian Family* in which Christenson minces no words about what a husband and wife must do. A wife must submit to her husband *completely*. A husband must *lay down his life* for his wife. Surely these words eliminate the slightest hope that things will be fair after all. The Bible teaches the same thing. The pattern is clear and consistent.

This was becoming more plain to us, but still we fought back. Our discussions, more often like heated debates, were taking a new turn. We struggled for workable answers to what lay before us. At least now our talks were honest. We questioned, debated, and defended ourselves, gaining occasional insight and often sinking into frustration. I insisted that Judy give up her earlier goals and plans and demanded the same commitment of myself.

As time wore on the strain intensified for Judy. The commitment required of her was clearly more visible, more overt, and therefore more difficult. She argued and questioned. Her honest heart and godly spirit wanted the practical truth. No half truths. No pat answers. What does it mean for a woman to leave her parents and be joined, be "one," with her husband?

The climax came one morning before I left for the store. Once more it was the "leader, authority, spiritual head" part of me counseling Judy about the necessity of her laying down her independent interests. She, in the emotion of the moment, only able to see the imperfect "me" groping right along with her, resisted.

"But why do I have to change and quit all these things when you can still do everything you've always done?"

Realizing that Judy's immediate need was not to hear a defense of the equality of my efforts, I tried calmly to resist the temptation to one more argument.

"It's not a matter of what I'm doing—" I began.

"I don't see why," interrupted Judy. "Why is it always *me*?"

"It isn't always you," I answered. "But right now we're talking about the things you're facing. That doesn't have anything to do with me."

Now in tears, Judy rebutted, "We're always talking about me! I have to give everything up even if you don't change a thing! Is it all my fault? Does everything depend on my giving up these things I enjoy?"

"Yes," I answered, trying to give her the guidance she needed as her leader rather than the emotional answer of an involved husband. "I suppose from your side it does all depend on you. You can't ask yourself what I'm doing. That's between me and the Lord. You just have to lay down your own life, regardless of me."

And in a final outburst of frustration and anguish, she blurted out, *"But it's not fair!"*

"Judy," I answered, "it's not supposed to be fair!"

The words were hard and cold, jolting us both like icy water in the face.

* * *

Through those words God gave us the key to what lay ahead. The following day saw a new spirit. Through the words God had put in my mouth, many of our questions disappeared. Judy called the orchestra leader and withdrew from the fall performances. She called the church and said she'd not be able to continue being in charge of the Bible school program. Within the week we'd also decided for her not to go back to school for the final semester of her credential work.

The fog began to lift.

2

X Rays and Tests

"What is a 'mole,' anyway?" Judy asked.

We were sitting of the edge of our bed poring over a huge nursing obstetrics book we had borrowed from a friend. It was the evening of the doctor's fateful phone call. We looked up "mole" and scanned the page over and over. It was certainly a grim possibility and the pictures only made it worse. In layman's language a mole is a growth inside the uterus which displays many of the symptoms of pregnancy but which is completely unrelated. It increases in size at about the same rate so confusion often exists. What it actually is, I could never figure out. A consistency "like tapioca" the doctor said. In earlier times moles were occasionally cancerous and proved fatal. Now, however, their removal was considered routine. "Don't worry," the doctor had said. *Don't worry!* I thought. *How does he expect me not to worry?*

Other frightening words and hints were scattered through the brief article. Words such as "hysterectomy." The doctor never mentioned these extreme possibilities and probably there was no danger, but keeping one's mind from wandering back to the "worst" is usually impossible.

That night there was nothing to do but wait. We did our best to trust God. We knew He was in charge, but transferring that knowledge into feelings was another matter.

Earlier in the day there had been some additional things which contributed to the memorable series of events. Shortly after Judy's urine test and X ray, her father walked into the store. This was an unexpected shock since her family lived eight hundred miles away. He had been forced to take a brief leave of absence from his school position due to illness and had driven north to see his two daughters in Oregon and northern California. His visit was timely. For the few days he was with us I sensed a depth in his relationship with Judy and knew that he was an added comfort and encouragement to her.

Judy's brother Doug had handcrafted a beautiful wooden cradle for our new baby which her father, Bob, brought up. We had heard about it and had long anticipated seeing it. On this particular day, however, it was hard to be excited. Having just been jolted by the news that there might not even be a baby there, it was hard to think about and plan to use a cradle.

It was a long night. We anxiously awaited what we hoped would be good news the next day. And when the doctor did finally notify us the cloud lifted slightly. Thursday's urine test showed a noticeably lower level. It was still above normal, but definitely showed the chances of a mole to be lessening. The X-ray results, which hopefully would confirm positively what exactly was inside Judy's body, were still unavailable. Dr. Martin, therefore, in the absense of certain proof regarding the mole possibility, had decided to cancel the surgery. His uneasiness was still very clear to us as he groped for options to explain the unusual factors involved.

"The only other thing I can think of," he went on, thinking aloud more than offering a professional hypothesis, "is that the baby has died somewhere along the line. Of course there's no way to know that for sure, but it would explain the weight gain."

"How is that?" I weakly asked.

"If the baby died," the doctor continued, "the body

would keep producing liquids just as if the pregnancy were normal. The baby, of course, would be unable to use them, so they would just continue to build up without being disposed of."

"But then what about the urine test? Would there be any relation to it?"

"Well, no, there wouldn't. And that's the problem with the idea, it simply wouldn't explain the two tests."

After a pause he went on, noticeably just grasping for any suggesting to explain the high test results.

"But I'm still wondering if that first test indicated a severe imbalance that might not have just been a fluke."

"How could that be?"

"The lab can make mistakes. It has happened."

"But if that were true, then the second test should have been normal," I pursued.

"Well, that's true. Frankly, I just don't know what to make of it. We'll just have to wait for the X-ray results on Monday."

As I hung up the phone, my fleeting joy that the surgery had been cancelled had all but disappeared. The doctor was in such obvious doubt. I could feel the uncertainty in his voice.

Everything remained doubtful. The weekend dragged on—slowly. Judy and I gave God thanks for this blessing through trial, but it was out of obedience rather than joy. We knew that He had somehow chosen us to go through this. And we knew it was for our good and His honor. We also knew that we had to learn to be more joyful and more genuine in our thanks. But at the time, the "joy of the Lord" was far away. The uneasiness was hanging heavily on us.

Sunday at church the pastor called for prayer requests and healing. Judy and I with her father, Bob, went down to the altar along with many others to request prayer. Rus Connett, one of the elders, knelt down with us and asked about our need.

"There are some complications with Judy's pregnancy," I said.

Rus prayed simply and clearly, claiming complete health for Judy and the baby.

While he prayed it suddenly struck Judy how much she'd already given in to doubt. Having by now assumed that the baby, if there even was one, was dead, she found herself reacting to Rus' prayer.

How can you pray for the "health" of a dead baby? she thought.

It was clear we both had much to learn about thankfulness through this. The Lord was dealing with us and it was painful.

The following day the X rays were due. "At last we'll know!" we assured ourselves.

Judy took the day off from teaching. She spent most of the day at the store with me, waiting. Every time the phone rang we started and looked apprehensively at each other. But each call was just business—no Dr. Martin. Judy's father was preparing to leave for Oregon but was waiting until the X rays were in. The day wore on as if life and death hung in the balance. And, really, it did for us! Judy and Bob went over to the doctor's office and sat for an hour without learning a thing. Later in the day we called the office. "No results yet," we were politely informed.

Finally, the atmosphere was so intense and the waiting so ridiculous that Bob decided to leave. He would call us that night for any news. Unable to sit around any longer, Judy decided late in the day to go back to Dr. Martin's office and wait, no matter how long it took.

Finally the results arrived.

"There *is* a baby," Judy told me.

My reaction was not elation, but certainly relief. "There is no mole," I sighed to myself. But beyond that conclusion, the doctor was reluctant to draw anything further. There was no detectable heartbeat since

Judy was barely three months along. And the smallness of the baby did not correspond to Judy's size and weight. There was still too much uncertainty. The "dead baby" option now seemed to head the list of possibilities, and his doubts were all too clear. The brief encouragement was short-lived.

He scheduled Judy to see a specialist on the following Thursday, hoping to provide some answers where his limited knowledge of obstetrics failed. Another long week of waiting began.

* * *

During those next days we did considerable thinking and praying. It was clear that we were not behaving like people who had the Lord to trust in and lean upon. The long, anxious Monday disclosed beyond any doubt that we were carrying the burden ourselves rather than turning it over to Jesus. To Judy, that week it was made clear that her attempted thankfulness had been backwards. Hanging onto the verse, "If you confess with your mouth ...," it struck her that while trying to do that she had been ignoring the rest of the passage, "... and believe in your heart."

Though the process was slow, it was during that week the Lord began to get through to us a few elementary principles about *being* thankful. Naturally the start often must be made with a confession (which most likely has to ignore the way you feel at the time). But a proper heart attitude of genuine thankfulness to God for His utter goodness (again, despite the feelings of the moment) must accompany it.

As Judy began to make the effort to thank God from her heart, she began thinking about the death of Jesus, and what it must have signified to God, His Father. Her thoughts moved on to His death ... His resurrection ... His *victory* over death.

Suddenly it burst in on her.

"This unborn child belongs to you, Lord! *This child is yours!* To love ... to take ... or even to give us if you wish!"

And at that point a glimmer of true thankfulness began to flow from Judy's heart. It was thankfulness simply for the special love and goodness that God gives. The "glimmer" began to grow. Judy's heart began to lift, and mine with it.

During the remainder of that week, God brought us through the worst of our doubts into a place where we were able to start rightly thanking Him. It wasn't our own doing, for in ourselves all we seemed able to do was doubt and worry. But the fact that God had put it in our hearts made it no less real.

LOVE

He has granted to us His exceeding great and precious promises . . . —2 Pet. 1:4 (author's par.)

Take delight in the Lord, and he will give you the desires of your heart.—Ps. 37:4 (RSV)

The Christian should have more vividly expressed creativity in his daily life, and have more creative freedom, as well as the possibility of a continuing development in creative activities.[1]

The freedom and creativity and fruitfulness God intends to pour forth from the love relationship between a man and woman can come about only when authority and submission are properly understood and put into practice. When husband and wife do accept and begin to function in their godly roles, many exciting things begin to happen. Their love for one another increases and begins to bear fruit in many areas. And God is able to bless them with children born of His promise and raised in His love.

3

Expanding Vision

Our marriage had weathered an earlier crisis. And then, as now, the way out of the gloom into the sunlight of God's blessing was through giving of thanks. Upon realizing that "it's not supposed to be fair," a period followed during which Judy and I had to just grin and thankfully bear it. Like it or not, we both saw that laying down our earlier goals was the only way to fully accept and live according to the new priorities God was showing us. He had given us substantial insight on how to remake our marriage into the miracle we had earlier known it would be. But there were few overnight changes. We tried (in obedience, not because we always felt like it) to put the other one first.

Judy began a dedicated effort to submit herself to me. For her this meant a rearrangement of many past priorities. It meant that her relationship with me, our home, the store, were now to be her life, rather than unrelated outside activities. For me the changes were similar—Judy and my time with her, my activities around the house, my evenings with her at home became what I threw myself into. My outside endeavors were greatly reduced.

Looking back on this period Romans 1:21 stands out as the beacon light which guided us out of the woods. "Although they knew God they ... did not give thanks

to Him...and their minds were darkened." We had
failed to give God thanks in our marriage and the inevitable result followed. Now, though our emotions still had
to be healed of much hurt, we determined to give God
the thanks due Him. We were solidly together on that
single point. We *must* thank God—always.

Francis Schaeffer offered much guidance during this
time, especially through *True Spirituality*. I read it over
three times in succession, determined not to let its message pass by.

> A quiet disposition and a heart giving thanks at any
> given moment is the real test of the extent to which we
> love God at that moment...it must be giving thanks
> for ALL things—this is God's standard.
>
> The beginning of men's rebellion against God was,
> and is, the lack of a thankful heart...trust and content-
> ment must be in the Christian framework...If the con-
> tentment goes and the giving of thanks goes, we are not
> loving God as we should...[this] is the first place of
> loss of true spirituality.[2]

Not only did this give me insight into what had happened in our marriage, it also pointed the way to the
solution. It was a great benefit to my understanding.

Still it was months of "three steps ahead, two back."
We easily forgot to give thanks, went back on our resolu-
tions, and let ourselves think of those things we missed.
We still had long and sometimes "warm" discussions.
The difficulties between us weren't altogether eliminated
by any means. But I think we both were aware of being
on the same road together for the first time. Our rough
edges rubbed together, but there was a mutual willingness
to "give thanks anyway" and to make the adjustments
necessary. Now that we had a clearer picture of our distinct roles, it was just a matter of time and practice
before those roles began to come naturally to us.

And, in time, living according to the scriptural roles
we knew God had ordained began to come with less effort.
We began to relate to each other as husband and wife

rather than as two active Christians. Growing within me was a new and different thankfulness for Judy. No longer did I have to give thanks for her simply because God commanded it. He began to show me many facets of her personality which had been hidden before. Whether this was due to my blindness or the fact that her talents had been surpressed, I don't know. Undoubtedly both my new attitude toward Judy and her new commitment to our marriage contributed to this flowering of much that was within her. But I truly began to see and appreciate this "virtuous woman," or as the literal meaning in Proverbs 31 has it, "a woman of many parts." That was my Judy. Many gifts and abilities showed themselves. A productivity and creativity surfaced that I had not seen. Like the woman described in Proverbs, her abilities were now being used in our home and for the sake of our marriage.

Most of these things which I now noticed in Judy were small. She took a renewed interest in the house. She spent time in the yard. There were often flowers in a vase, and the atmosphere in our home began to reflect Judy and came alive. Any words to describe it sound superficial, but to me it was like the difference between waking up to a cold, foggy morning and waking up to sunlight through the window and birds chirping on a warm, sunny day. I know it was more than simply my changing attitude toward things. There was a sunlight in our home and it was being expressed through Judy.

What was happening was the miracle of a woman settling into her rightful place in God's order of creation. Only in perfect submission can a woman develop and mature in the status and dignity granted her by the God who created her. When this happens a woman is enabled to move about with great freedom and creativity. This I witnessed in Judy. Her submission to me in practical areas—music playing when I came home from work, fixing a "special" breakfast for me, walking part way down to the store to meet me on my way home, bringing me a present, being interested in my interests, going all out to please me, sharing my excitement with the store, even watching a football game with me—made me all the more eager to give her anything she desired. I found my "authority" over her to be more low key all the time because of the trust and confidence I had in her. When a husband and wife are flowing in headship and submission as God intended, there is little of the domineering and cowering traits so often associated with these words when improperly understood. True authority and submission is the only way for a husband and wife really to be free to love one another totally.

We found ourselves being led into new areas of ministry—this time together. God seemed to move in both of us simultaneously now. As the leader I would often be the one to propose something, but Judy's response would indicate that she too had been thinking along similar lines. One Sunday afternoon as we were talking about the store and its future, God suddenly moved in a dramatic way. He flashed on us both a vision of the ministry of our store in coming years—a greatly expanded ministry, many times beyond what we had ever imagined before. It was a glimpse of what *He* intended to do in and through our store. We were *excited*!

But the most significant thing was that He gave us both this vision—*together*. It wasn't *my* vision for the future of the store. It had come to the two of us. We were becoming one, Judy and I, in God's design and plan.

Another aspect of this new "togetherness" was in re-opening our home to others. We had now been living alone for quite some time. But through our new relationship, God began to put into each of us a desire to have people in our home. This time, however, it didn't take the form of having people living with us, but having people over for dinner or for the afternoon. We would invite people from other churches and friends we hadn't seen for some time. God used these occasions for people to fellowship who might otherwise never have been involved together.

It was a ministry of entertaining, of providing fellowship. We felt it was a ministry He had given us. We did not invite *my* friends or *her* friends. It was something we shared, and somehow this too brought us that much closer.

Throughout the following two years God brought to fulfillment much of what He had shown us about the store. We moved into a building about four times as large and the business continued to expand rapidly. The store began to have a noticeable affect in the community, and especially the Christian community. The record album "Come Together" by Jimmy Owens and Pat Boone was released, and it expressed much of the "vision" Judy and I had been shown earlier. The record's impact on the Christians in our area coincided remarkably with the growth and similar impact of our store. God was moving. He was bringing together His people in completely new ways. Barriers were breaking down between churches and between individuals.

I mention these things not to incorporate a separate story but because to me they are a direct outcome of the new relationship between Judy and me. I know that for God to carry out His will in our store, He had to get Judy and I squared away toward each other. He could not use a broken vessel. His moving in so many aspects of our lives further demonstrated to me that He was responsible for what we had come through and was guiding us into authority and submission and their fruitful benefits.

People who balk at the mention of basing a marriage on biblical principles do not understand that God is unable to use to the fullest two people who are trying to do it their own way. There is just no other way for God to bless a marriage and use it as He designed. Each time I pause to reflect on our marriage before we knew our proper roles, praise to God wells up inside me. I know that I did not have the wisdom necessary to pull us out of that hole. I would never have thought of arranging a marriage as God does. I thank Him that He never stops teaching a willing and listening ear, that He kept my ears open and kept Judy's love for me strong.

I give much of the credit for these changes in our marriage to Judy. Her willingness overwhelms me to this day. Had I been standing where she was I am not at all sure I would have been able to submit to the changes she did. Marabel Morgan is correct when she says in *The Total Woman* that women have the power to change a marriage and turn it around. "It is possible ... for almost any wife to have her husband absolutely adore her in just a few weeks' time. She can revive romance, reestablish communication, break down barriers, and put sizzle back into her marriage. It is really up to her. She has the power." [3]

I agree. And I personally bear witness to it. I do adore my wife. Her complete willingness to follow me and bear with me had its perfect results. Not only did it get our marriage flowing again, it made me more open to express my love for her. In my new role I found that I had an increased freedom also. With my leadership firmly established, both because I held it firmly and because Judy submitted to it, there was no more pressure on me. There was an increased freedom all around.

Accompanying Judy's changing interest in the things concerning our home was a corresponding awakening in my spirit. Both Judy's creativity—it seemed as if she could suddenly *do* so many things—and the book by Edith Schaeffer, *Hidden Art*, stimulated a hunger within me to be artistic. I don't mean to paint or to draw, or to sculpture, but to be artistic and creative as a person with many varied capabilities.

I didn't know how to fix a car, build a cabinet, fix a leak, or plant a garden. But I found growing inside me an enthusiasm to learn—about all kinds of things. I wanted to be creative with my hands. I had always so admired my father's seemingly "infinite" knowledge about everything. But now I saw that creativity, the ability to do, make, design, was built into every man. And God could bring it to the surface.

Again, why mention this? Because to me it was an additional indication of the changes God was bringing about. A new appreciation for God's creation was turning me from always wanting to "do" to wanting simply to "see" and give thanks to God. I began to "behold" flowers and plants, and God used them to teach me about His character. Little things caught my attention. God's order, beauty, and creativity were literally *everywhere*.

My home life, rather than my activities, was becoming the arena of my commitment. Sitting outside pulling weeds together, painting the house, paneling a wall, hanging a picture—these were important to Judy and me because we did them together. We did not see our "spiritual" life as something removed from these "mundane" affairs. No. We saw that God was truly in every facet of life. To us, taking pride in our yard was deeply woven into our commitment to God. Watching a TV program together was also of God. The "externals" became secondary to us. It was what was going on *inside* that mattered. Still ever on our minds was giving thanks. If while planting gladiola bulbs in the yards, we could thank God for the dirt, the sun, the worm, and the dandelion—then we were spiritually in a more sound position than if we'd been attending meeting after meeting. Even though preaching and praising and singing may have been going on around us, if our hearts were not thankful it would mean nothing. It is not the circumstances or the geographical situation but the attitude that's important.

God was bringing us these new priorities about Him and showing us what true worship of Him is (a thankful heart in all things) largely through our renewed commitment to one another. Our emphasis on our home life, almost to a self-centered degree, was necessary for Him to disentangle our minds from years of being trained in externals rather than heart attitudes.

So we had to withdraw, center down our lives on our attitudes of learning to give Him thanks. And in so doing God nurtured a creativity which comes from seeing Him in everything. That is the nature of true creativity, you know—seeing God in everything that is before you.

One morning is especially memorable. I had left for the store and was about three blocks from home. I was thinking how totally every little thing was something God had made. I was appreciating the sunshine, the morning, the smells, the walk. I was expressing to the Lord my desire to be able to express His character and love through my personality, through things I made, through the store. There was welling up inside me an extreme desire to create and demonstrate the love of God with my hands. And at the same time my heart was just bursting in thanks to God for having *himself* created so much and given it all to us.

Then out loud I was almost surprised to hear myself say, "Lord, I just want to be a totally integrated, creative person! Let my life express your creativity."

That prayer so perfectly expressed the life Judy and I shared during this special time in our marriage. From the table I made on the porch to the biscuits she made at dinner—God used it all to teach us thankfulness and to deepen our love for one another. He answered this prayer largely through my wife. Her love for me allowed something to bloom which might otherwise forever have remained dormant. And in the same way I know my new commitment to Judy allowed her a freedom to become the creative woman of God she was showing herself to be. It is wonderful what hidden treasures are uncovered when a man and woman choose to love each other totally in obedience to God's design.

4

Preparing for Parenthood—
Do the Principles Work?

Having been so thoroughly occupied with activities, plans and "service," Judy and I had given little thought to children during the early years of our marriage. Then later the desperate attempt to solidify our relationship continued to keep a family out of our immediate consideration. Even though I had taught school and Judy was preparing to do so, and though Judy had always been active in children's church groups, we were married without ever having discussed children of our own.

Once our lives began to flow somewhat more smoothly, however, and the anxiety and conflict gave way to the love and anticipation of being a "family," children began to penetrate our thoughts. Starting a family was the next natural step in the new home-family oriented priorities the Lord was giving us. As Judy and I desired to give ourselves more totally to one another, having a baby became a mutual desire.

By this time Judy was back in school finalizing her credential work. I was giving serious thought about her teaching the following term. So it was necessary for us to do some very serious and practical thinking about having a baby. It was certain she couldn't have a baby midway through the school year. When a job opened at the Christian School in Arcata, we decided to have Judy apply and wait until after the school year to have our baby. When interviewed by the school board for the job, Judy plainly said she might be pregnant for a good part of the year. She was hired for the job nevertheless.

God is a master at tying things together. What appear to us to be disconnected events are vitally linked strands in His marvelous plan. This is one reason we are told to thank Him for everything—because in every detail His perfect plan for our life is being worked out. He leaves nothing out.

Romans 8:28 never ceases to drive this home. "We know that all things work together for our good when we are in God's will and living according to His plan for us." *All things are for our good.* God overlooks nothing!

We were seeing God at work preparing us for our baby—whenever the time came. In working the changes He had in our marriage, His constant promise had been, "Trust me. I'll make this more marvelous than either of you ever dreamed." Even when we were at the bottom, that promise returned to us. Hannah Hurnard's Shepherd kept the vision alive with words like:

> All my servants on their way to the High Places have had to make this detour through the desert. . . . Here they have learned about things which otherwise they would never have known about. . . . With tears of anguish an endless succession of My people have come this way. You too, are in the line of succession. It is a great privilege. . . . Those who come down to the furnace go their way afterwards as royal men and women, princes and princesses of the Royal Line.[1]

As the time approached for Judy and me to enlarge our family, we could see that God had been carrying out a long process of preparation in our hearts for what was to follow. Judy's first- and second-grade class was to provide one of the most striking examples.

One contributing factor in our decision for Judy to teach was in what her experience could teach us both as we looked ahead to parenthood. The laws of our country

require an enormous amount of formal and apprentice-
ship training before allowing a person to practice skills
in most fields. This is often up to eighteen or twenty
years, depending on the efficiency and preparation
necessary. But to raise a child, not a day of training
is given. A man and woman can produce a child without
the slightest knowledge of the principles of child-growth
and development, nutrition, or discipline. Somehow it is
assumed that it will "come naturally" and that love is
enough to see unprepared parents through the early for-
midable years. But as James Dobson says, "The mistakes
they make are certainly unintentional, yet the consequences are no less severe." [2]

Judy and I were aware that having a child would bring
us face to face with an array of "unknowns." We had
entered our marriage unsuspecting and unprepared for
the problems and adjustments we were to encounter. And
in our naïveté our marriage came uncomfortably close
to splitting apart. Now we faced what possibly would
be even greater changes and adjustments. If we had
learned from our past experiences together, it was
to do our best to anticipate and prepare for what might
lay ahead. We knew that "prepared" was something one
could never fully become. But we also knew that this
is no reason for not being as prepared as possible. We
had seen the advent of children drastically change many
marriages and relationships, often in a negative way.
A couple would have a child and then the woman would
withdraw into the life of her child while the husband continued his previous life-style largely alone. After cheer-
fully deciding to have a child, the parents would begin
to resent this child having forced them out of an "active"
life into one of diapers and sleepless nights.

So we determined to be prepared as best we could,
knowing full well that we would be caught many times
asking, "What do we do now?" It is the mature couple,
having given their marriage thought and planning, who
are able to cope with the unexpected when it comes, not

the teenagers whose marriage was a lark. And in the same way we felt it was the knowledgeable and thoughtful parents who would be able to weather the later shocks and bumps with the least trauma. In our reading and discussing there was little of our earlier idealism which said, "*We'll* have no problems!" We knew we would have plenty. But the more resources we had at our disposal, the more confidence we had in our ability to handle them.

So we read, discussed, tried to work out hypothetical situations and grew more and more excited over the prospect of actually having a child of our own. But in our anticipation we desired practical reassurance concerning many of the principles we studied. This was especially true in the area of discipline. What a hot topic that is! There are as many theories about discipline in the home and classroom as there are books on the subject. We were sure that discipline played a vital role in the family structure, especially after we understood something about authority and God's design for its application.

We had read many theories, often directly conflicting with each other:

> A spanking... is patterned after our relationship to the Heavenly Father.... God did not intend spanking to be the last line of defense for an embattled parent. It is the *first* action which a parent takes, *in obedience to God*....[3]

> What is wrong with spanking is the lesson it demonstrates. It teaches children undesirable methods of dealing with frustrations.[4]

> When you are defiantly challenged, win decisively. When the child asks "Who's in charge?" tell him.[5]

> Spanking should be the last resort.[6]

However, with the exception of several months of part-time teaching I had done where spanking was not allowed, neither Judy nor I had any long-term experience in practicing these principles. We really wanted to know in a practical way which theories actually worked. We hoped that Judy's teaching would give us some answers.

The basic issue in our minds was this: To what extent must an adult (parent or teacher) insist that he is the one to set the boundaries, establish the rules, enforce the limits? Permissive theorists say a child must be free and restrictions should be minimal. Writers on the other end of the spectrum say a child's only true freedom comes from being forced to submit to well-defined limits and being disciplined whenever those limits are challenged. Most of the Christian writers we had studied were of the second school (Christenson, Dobson, Adams), but even among Christian writers the feelings were far from unanimous. We agreed in theory with the tendency toward strong discipline, but knew we had to test these ideas in actual situations. The upcoming school year, therefore, took on a special meaning. We knew that the discipline methods we would use on our own child would largely be formulated through the trial-and-error situations faced by Judy in her classroom.

During the latter part of the summer Judy and I drilled and questioned one another in the principles of discipline, largely using as our model Dobson's books *Dare to Discipline* and *Hide or Seek*. I considered Dobson's approach to be fairly middle-of-the-road, advocating spanking very strongly in only certain unique cases—in the moments of direct challenge to authority. Some teach not to spank. Others say to spank often. Dobson simply said to reserve the spanking for the moment when your authority is directly challenged. When consistently done in this manner, Dobson stresses that far fewer spankings actually must be given in the long run.

In most classroom situations spanking is not allowed, but the principle remains the same—set the limits and make sure that any child who challenges them (and your authority in the process) loses big. Judy would be fortunate since the Christian school did allow spanking. That would make potential discipline somewhat easier. But ever on our minds was the question, "Will it really work?" "What if we consistently try to apply Dobson's principles and the class is chaotic?''

But it was better to find out now than after we were struggling with our own child, we concluded.

Judy specifically primed herself mentally for that first time she would encounter a willful defiance of her authority by one of her new students. That would be the time when everything would be on the line. Judy must win that first encounter decisively to establish that she was in charge for the rest of the year. It was not her intention to establish a repressive atmosphere where her students feared her. On the contrary, it was our hope that by opening the year with the lines of authority and obedience clearly drawn, a classroom atmosphere of love and freedom would be created. This process and its frightful opposite are skillfully portrayed by James Dobson in his sketch of two teachers:

> On the first day of school in September, the new teacher, Miss Peach, gives the class a little talk which conveys this message: "I'm so glad we had a chance to get together. This is going to be such a fun year for you; we're going to make soap, and soup, and we're going to paint a mural that will cover that entire wall. We'll take field trips and play games ... this is going to be a great year. You're going to love me and I'm going to love you, and we'll just have a ball." Her curriculum is well saturated with fun, fun, fun activities, which are her tokens of affection to the class. All goes well the first day of school, because the students are a little intimidated by the start of a new academic year. But about three days later, little Butch is sitting over at the left, and he wants to know what everyone else is questioning, too: how far can we push Miss Peach? He is anxious to make a name for himself as a brave toughie, and he might be able to build his reputation at Miss Peach's expense. At a well-calculated moment he challenges her with a small act of defiance. Now the last thing Miss Peach wants is conflict because she had hoped to avoid that sort of thing this year. She does not accept Butch's challenge; she pretends not to notice that he didn't do what she

told him to do. He wins the first minor issue. Everyone in the class saw what happened; it wasn't a big deal but Butch survived unscathed. The next day, Matthew has been greatly encouraged by Butch's success. Shortly after the morning flag salute, he defies her a little more openly than Butch did, and Miss Peach again ignores the challenge. From that moment forward, chaos begins to grow and intensify. Two weeks later Miss Peach is beginning to notice that things are not going very well. She's doing a lot of screaming each day and she doesn't know how it got started; she certainly didn't intend to be a violent teacher. By February, life has become intolerable in her classroom; every new project she initiates is sabotaged by her lack of control. And then the thing she wanted least begins to happen: the students openly reveal their hatred and contempt for her. They call her names; they laugh at her weaknesses. If she has a physical flaw, such as a large nose or poor eyesight, they point this out to her regularly. Miss Peach cries quietly at recess time, and her head throbs and pounds late into the night. The principal comes in and witnesses the anarchy, and he says, "Miss Peach, you must get control of that class!" But Miss Peach doesn't know how to get control because she doesn't know how she lost it. . . .

Consider the contrasting approach of the skillful teacher, Mrs. Justice. She wants the love of the class too, but she is more keenly aware of her responsibility to the students. On the first day of school she delivers her inaugural address, but it is very different from the one being spoken by Miss Peach. She says, in effect, "This is going to be a good year, and I'm glad you are my students. I want you to know that each one of you is important to me. I hope you will feel free to ask your questions, and enjoy learning in this class; I will not allow anyone to laugh at you, because it hurts to be laughed at. I will never embarrass you intentionally, and I want to be your friend. But there's one thing you should know: if you choose to challenge me I have one thousand ways to make you miserable. If you don't believe me, you just let me know and we'll start with number one. Your parents have given me the responsibility of teaching you some very important things this year, and I have to get you ready for the knowledge you will learn next year. That's why I can't let one or two show-off's keep me from doing my job. We have got a lot to learn, so I think we'd better get started. Please get out your math books and turn to page four." About three days later, Butch's counterpart is on the job (there's at least one Butch in every classroom; if the classroom antagonist leaves during the year, a new demagogue will emerge to prominence). He challenges Mrs. Justice in a cautious manner, and she socks it to him. He loses big! Everyone in the class gets the message: it doesn't pay to attack Mrs. J. Wow! This poor Butch didn't do so well, did he? Mrs. Justice then proceeds to follow a little formula that I favor (tongue in cheek): don't smile 'til Thanksgiving. By November, this competent teacher has made her point. The class knows she's tougher, wiser, and braver than they are. Then she can begin to enjoy the pleasure of this foundation. She can loosen her control; the class can laugh together, talk together, and play together. But when Mrs. Justice says, "It's time to get back to work," they do it because they know she is capable of enforcing her suggestion. She does not scream. She does not hit. In fact, she can pour out the individual affection that most children need so badly. The class responds with deep love that will never be forgotten in those thirty-two lives. Mrs. Justice has harvested the greatest source of satisfaction available in the teaching profession: awareness of profound influence on human lives.[7]

5

"It Works!"

September came. Judy left for her first day at school with all the confidence of Mrs. Justice. She was ready to not be intimidated. What a shock when she walked into her new classroom and found it contained nine active and rambunctious little *boys*! All her dreams of teaching little girls (at least a *few,* anyway!) to dance and sing were gone in an instant. Instead it was to be muddy shoes, wrestling on the floor, and hiking in the woods. Well, be that as it may, authority and discipline must still be maintained.

It didn't take even three days for Butch (whose name happened to be David) to rear his head in defiance. Midway through the first day Judy said, "Okay, boys. Let's all come and sit down on the rug."

They all complied, with the exception of David who hung back.

"David," repeated Judy, "come on over. We're all going to sit down together."

"I don't want to get my new pants dirty," offered David in excuse.

"I'll clean them off after school if they get dirty," said Judy. "Now come over and sit down."

David set his feet, placed his hands on his hips, and firmly insisted, "No!"

That was it. He had challenged Judy's authority quickly and clearly. Sixteen other eyes were glued on Judy. What would she do? It was vital to each of them to know how far she could be pushed. David had chosen to be the one to help spell it out.

Judy calmly got up, picked up the alder switch we had cut for this specific moment, and decisively swatted David's little bottom.

He sat down, pouting.

Judy had demonstrated exactly what Mrs. Justice had shown—that she was capable of enforcing her words. Even though the first day of school was still in progress, the most significant disciplinary action of the year had just taken place. In that moment, Judy's class saw that disobedience did not pay off.

There were other acts of disobedience, but it did not take the class long to realize who was in control. Judy found it necessary to use her "rod" very rarely after that first day. Once her authority was clearly established, the class rarely chose to challenge it. Occasionally one of the boys would resist, testing the limits, just to make certain the authority was still there. But when he found Judy consistently enforcing her boundaries, the class would quickly return to normal.

Having firmly laid a foundation of authority in her classroom, Judy was now free to communicate confidence and self-worth to each one of the boys on a personal level. Consistent discipline is a basic ingredient to the building of self-esteem. In building a relationship with each boy, in spending time with every one, Judy taught them that they all were individually important to her. This in turn gave the boys a mutual respect and concern for one another, as a family. Rather than spending a lot of time on "spiritual" things, Judy's main effort was to treat each boy (and see that they treated one another) as a valuable person. And she was firmly convinced that her only success in doing this came about because she initially spelled out her authority and then stuck to it.

The building of self-esteem is one of the primary goals

of a teacher. But it can come about only if that teacher is fully maintaining his authority through discipline. Discipline enables a teacher to be free to teach many, many things. Judy's class expressed a happiness and creativity in knowing their rightful place under her leadership. Even when disciplined, a boy would usually exhibit a new joy soon afterward.

A child feels secure when there are well-defined limits about him. There is safety in boundaries. Children have an inborn sense of guidelines, order, justice. They know when they deserve to be disciplined. And they want to be disciplined. Children want the boundaries to remain firm and they test them only to make certain they are there. The more flexible and inconsistent the boundaries, the more a child needs to test and challenge them—not because he is rebellious but because he is insecure without that circle of protection.

> Children love justice. When someone has violated a rule, [and I maintain this includes the person himself] they want immediate retribution. They admire a teacher who can enforce an equitable legal system and they find a great comfort in reasonable social rules. By contrast the teacher who does not control her class, inevitably allow[ing] crime to pay, violate[s] something basic in the value system of children. . . . Children admire strict teachers because chaos is nerve-wracking. Screaming and hitting and wiggling are fun for about ten minutes; then the confusion begins to get tiresome and irritating.[1]

Many times Judy observed that the student she had recently been forced to discipline was the one coming to her anxious to express his boyish affection. On one occasion David (again) refused to do his work. It was an assignment he could easily have handled, but he just stubbornly refused to do it. As lunchtime approached, Judy made it clear to David that he would have to stay in until his assignment was completed. Still he sat doing nothing. When time for lunch did come, Judy left David at his seat crying over his unfinished paper, still hoping Judy would give in.

Five minutes later, however, David walked over to the other side of the room with his completed assignment. In the time it took to walk across the room to get his lunch pail his cloud disappeared. Before leaving the room to eat his lunch, David came up to Judy with a big smile on his face. "Guess what happened this morning, Mrs. Phillips?"

It was over, she was his friend again. Judy had won the battle and David's spirit rejoiced. He hadn't wanted to be "in charge," but he had to *make sure* she still was. In recounting the incident to me later, Judy was excited. "Children want to be submitted to someone strongly in charge, in authority," she said. "They want boundaries clearly defined and stuck to. And they want clear discipline when those boundaries are crossed."

Not only are limits a source of security for children, the same is true of order, neatness, predictability. Judy recalls an instance toward the end of the day when she was standing back watching her class put away their things. They were bustling about the room tracking down their books, games, building blocks, construct-o-straws, crayons, and the like. Judy suddenly "beheld" their awareness of order and routine as they talked among themselves.

"This goes on the top shelf."

"No, James, that book goes on the right, not on the left."

"Here, Rodney, I know where that goes. I'll put it away."

"No, the blocks go in *this* box."

"Which cupboard are the Richard Scarry books in?"

"Over there to the left, with Dr. Suess."

They were very exacting, almost ruthless, in their scrutiny of the room. Everything had to be in its proper place. They took pride in it. It was their room and it was in order. "And the most amazing thing of all," concluded Judy in telling me about it, "is that it's nothing I taught them. It's just natural to them."

It is a myth that children want to be "free" to do whatever they choose, whenever they choose. They were not meant to live that way and when left to themselves, do not choose to do so. On their own, children are quick to seek out order. Chaos is unnerving to them.

Dr. Lee Salk has noticed this:

> All children enjoy games because they absolutely adore the idea of engaging in an activity that has pattern and predictability.... They constantly try to find out exactly what the rules and regulations are.... Many times I have observed a group of three- or four-year-old children left to play in a room. Within minutes they organize activities that have rules and regulations... they start a game which is one method of finding out about each other by interacting in a predictable way... children search for life's rules.... They constantly test the world, exploring what makes things happen, if they happen consistently... children like the discipline of a game. It comes naturally, and so it can be with discipline in general.[2]

I am reminded of an experiment described by Dr. Dobson which attempted to allow children more freedom by removing the order and boundaries which they were accustomed to.

> During the early days of the progressive education movement, one enthusiastic theorist decided to take down the chain-link fence that surrounded the nursery school yard. He thought the children would feel more freedom of movement without that visible barrier surrounding them. When the fence was removed, however, the boys and girls huddled near the center of the play yard. Not only did they not wander away, they didn't even venture to the edge of the grounds.
>
> There is security in defined limits. When the home atmosphere is as it should be, the child lives in utter safety. He never gets in trouble unless he deliberately asks for it, and as long as he stays within the limits, there is mirth and freedom and acceptance.[3]

Well, we were certainly finding the principles (which

previously had been mostly theory to us) to be working! Christenson said, "Children thrive on set order and routine." [4] Dobson said, "Discipline and love are not antithetical; one is a function of the other." [5] Larry Richards said, "The whole meaning of discipline is much closer to 'guidance' . . . " [6] Dobson again said, in effect, "Good discipline is vital to building self-esteem." [7] We had read. We had studied. Now, through Judy's classroom, we were discovering that *it works*!

That does not mean having a pocketful of theories overcame every situation. There were also obstacles which completely confounded us both—Judy in the classroom and me at home later hearing about it. One day Judy entered the classroom to find a dilemma which could only have been instigated by one person—Dickie. When confronted with it, he denied it emphatically. Throughout the day he stuck to his conviction that he was innocent. But it remained clear to Judy that he was responsible.

What could she do? He had lied to her before. Do you accuse him of lying right to his face and run that fraction-of-1-percent risk that he was in the clear after all? Do you force the truth out of the other children, even though to do so might create further hostilities between themselves? How is it possible to "win," keeping your authority intact? Discipline was clearly called for, but there is no formula which fits the situation. She never did figure out what should have been done.

These perplexing situations came up frequently. It is just impossible to box up the theories in such a way that they provide you with a nice neat solution every time. Theories must be lived out in daily life among people. And people, especially children, are not predictable. Your convictions must carry a built-in flexibility if they are to stand up with time and practice. That is no reason to discard theories, but it certainly means we must keep the convictions at the root of our theories strong. Only in so doing will the practical outworking of our principles have the flexibility to cope with ever-changing, always different circumstances.

Judy's relationships with her boys kept her constantly thinking and constantly asking, "What should I do with Clinton? Chris and Mark are so close, are they having trouble responding to a woman teacher after last year? How should I have handled that situation between Rodney and David? How can I help Kelly? I don't know how his brother is affecting Jimmy."

It was a tremendous year of preparation for both of us because we were well aware that many of these "no-solution" problems would come up in later years with our own children. It forced us to deal with things as they arose. We never got to the point of feeling on top of it. New challenges came up quickly and no two were ever alike. In the end we both agreed that our basic plan for dealing with children was simply to keep well up on the general principles so we were able to spontaneously and quickly deal with straightforward problems such as outright defiance of authority. Beyond that it is simply necessary to stay on your toes, pay attention, and be aware immediately when a new problem arises. If it doesn't fit any pattern, then sit down and think it out. Try to analyze what's going on in this case and arrive at an appropriate strategy to handle it. It isn't necessary to have everything down cold. But it is necessary to be clear-headed and attentive, watchful in a relaxed way.

* * *

Judy's year of teaching confirmed to us more strongly than ever that the principles of authority and discipline were true to the Bible. And, just as importantly, they worked in practice. Whatever doubts we had when school began were now gone. We knew we would make many mistakes with our own children, but we also had a strong confidence that in following the principles we had learned, we would be conforming to God's ordained way.

The very morning I began writing this section on classroom discipline, our pastor preached on spiritual authority and submission. His words once again confirmed the truth and timelessness of these principles. The message was clear: though many seem to think Christianity and the Bible to be founded on democratic principles, nothing in fact could be further from the truth. God's established pattern of dealing with men from the very beginning was through obedience to authority. To begin with, it was God's authority alone: "Do not eat the fruit from the tree. . . . " In the Garden there was only one rule. All obedience was centered around that one command. The blessings of obedience and the penalty of disobedience were clearly spelled out. When man disobeyed, God followed through.

After Adam, God appointed certain men to be in authority under Him. The children of Israel took no votes in deciding their course of action in leaving Egypt. Moses simply said, "Thus says the Lord." And Israel obeyed. Moses was God's authority. There were times when the whole congregation was against him. Moses did not weaken. He stood firm because the Lord's word was to be obeyed even if *everyone* disagreed. When Korah and Dathan and many of Israel's leading men rose against him, Moses did not defend himself. He simply took the matter to the Lord, who reaffirmed Moses to be His anointed over the people.

When the Israelites entered into the land of promise, God made it abundantly clear that two choices lay before them—obedience or disobedience. He stated the rules they were to live by and then outlined the blessings of obedience and the penalties for disobedience. It was all clearly detailed ahead of time. When they disobeyed years later, God carried out His word. The people were scattered and destroyed according to His exact promise. God's authority was absolute. Those who lived in obedience were blessed according to the promise also. Authority is not negative. It is solid, and as such has both positive and negative aspects, depending on the obedience to it.

And in New Testament times God appointed men within the church to rule over the larger body. God did not set up the church or the family democratically. He created man to be in submission to all those in authority—from God himself down to our fellowman. We were never created to be free unto ourselves.

This is one of the crucial areas where authority is misunderstood. We have a hazy and incorrect understanding of freedom. The world looks at freedom as total independence—no rules, no restrictions, no responsibilities. But the true freedom for which we were created is the freedom of being properly related in our hearts—to God, to our leaders, and to one another. Freedom, therefore, is interdependence, not independence. We were not made to live autonomous lives. When we try to, things eventually go wrong. We are made of the same breed as the children who could not be "free" without the boundaries around their playground. We were made to live within boundaries, under authority.

God's intention in creating us to live under His authority is not to keep us pinned down but to allow us to live fully free in His love. Once properly related to God under His authority, God intends to give us increasing freedom and responsibility. But in order to be fully effective, that responsibility must be channeled according to His will. So the submission to God's authority must come first. Then comes a freedom and responsibility as God's servant. Freedom will come no other way.

The message of authority and the necessity to live by its principles is found on nearly every page of the Bible. Through continued study of the Bible and again through excellent books (Watchman Nee's *Spiritual Authority* is one of the best), Judy and I continued to see our vital need to have authority working in our marriage and our home by the time a baby came. Dobson's books continued to be a strong influence and Judy's classroom the training ground for much of our reading.

Even though most of our customers are Christians,

we saw in our store what an appalling lack of control most parents have over their children. Ann Lander's words, "Parents are being guided by children . . . children are calling the signals. They are clearly in control," [8] were never so true as on a busy Saturday afternoon in our store—parents rushing about after their children from this to that, trying to keep them out of trouble. We encountered parental opposition to some of Judy's disciplining techniques (even such low-key measures as simply not backing down from student pressure). These things showed us that even though authority is taught in the Scriptures, most Christians still retain democratic feelings concerning authority. The American democratic way says, "What right do you have to lay down the law, saying, 'This is it!'?" (Even when such statements are from teachers toward their students and parents toward their children.) Christian parents often will not take this strong affirmative stance. As is clear from Scripture (and to us was now clear in practice), even though living by these principles of authority proved to be the best possible way to love and build faith and confidence into children, Christians still do not follow them.

To me the price of trying to raise children any other way is too high. Maintaining your authority with children may seem hard, but it is not nearly so hard as the tension that results when discipline is not consistently carried out. The child-controlled relationships we witness in our store have demonstrated this to me many times. Seeing distraught parents totally at the mercy of their children strengthened our convictions not to lose control and let our own children be in charge. We intended to retain that authority-submission balance.

The proof of the pudding is in the eating, and the proof of the theory is in the practice. We had begun our search into the nature and practice of parental authority some time earlier by trying to answer the simple question, "Does it work?"

When I looked at the results in Judy's classroom relationships, comparing it with other classrooms and with the child-controlled relationships I saw daily in our store, my answer had to be a resounding "Yes!" In other classrooms, without the strong sense of discipline and leadership, chaos and rebellion reigned. Then when I looked at Judy's room I saw contentment, peace, freedom to laugh and play, respect, and with these things, remarkable scholastic growth and development. The contrast was evident.

I also had to stand back and take a long look at our marriage. Why was it working now when it had been so devastated just two years earlier? I knew it had to be our changing attitude toward our roles and our attempted obedience to live according to God's authority. If nothing had happened as a result of my having tried to be the leader and authority in my home and Judy's willing and costly submission, then I would have wondered, "Is this whole business hogwash?"

But the fact is, it *was* working. Therefore I had no choice but to conclude that the principles are truthful, workable, and from God. The theories must be evaluated by the results. I needed no further convincing about the raising of my children. I knew these principles would act as my guidelines.

6

The Uncertain Months

As Judy's school year had progressed through the fall, we began to be more in earnest about having a baby. Each month we wondered, "Could this be the month?" Then in the second week of November Judy took a bad fall on the playground at school. Ame, the school secretary, expressed concern that it could well have caused a concussion. Judy was a little shaky for a few days but no treatment was given and she was fine before long.

But immediately on our minds as a result was the question, "What if Judy is pregnant? Could something have been done to harm the baby?" We had heard stories about injuring an unborn child, especially during the first critical months before the fetus becomes firmly attached to the uterus wall.

Aware of these dangers we waited with anxious interest, and as soon as was possible Judy went to the Health Department for a pregnancy test. And sure enough she was pregnant! God had answered our prayers. But even in our joy there was a tinge of apprehension. It is so easy to forget the promises and goodness of God.

I am inspired by Abraham, to whom God promised a son. Even after Isaac had been given to him, when God required him back again, Abraham gave him up in perfect faith. He knew that God was well able to raise his son from the dead if need be in order to fulfill the promise. God had also made a promise to Judy and me, as He had to Abraham, that He would make of our marriage something "more marvelous than we could have even dreamed." Yet when this obstacle reared its head, I responded in doubt.

"God . . . how can *you* be in this?"

Thankfulness did not flow from my heart as it should have. I was already forgetting "in *all* things give thanks, for this is God's perfect will for you." My mind occupied itself with all kinds of doubtful things, rather than "God is well able to go so far as raise the dead in order to fulfill His promises." But thank God, His faithfulness is not dependent upon our limited trust in Him. He is faithful regardless and carries out His promises in spite of our doubt.

However, these early doubts were minor (had we but seen what lay ahead we would have known how minor they *really* were) and gradually subsided. At Judy's first appointment with Dr. Martin, he seemed unconcerned about the fall so we gave it less thought ourselves. The anticipation of having a baby the following summer was heightened by the news that both my sister and Judy's sister were also expecting a couple of months ahead of us. God once again opened the way for us to have two young people live with us. (This time it was *really* a team effort since our own relationship was in order.) Clarry and Mary moved in with us the early months of the new year and they were a tremendous help in easing the housekeeping load from Judy's shoulders.

* * *

In February, the daughter of our close friends Charlie and Janice McCann, baby Angela, suddenly died. Her birth six months earlier had been surrounded with doubt and suffering. The numerous physical defects, long hospital visits and emergency operations really woke us up to the fact that pregnancy and birth are not to be taken for granted. Every healthy child born is a gift from

God. Yet even Angela's short, sad life was miraculously used by God. There was much rejoicing over her life and great blessing even in her death. Even so, it caused Judy and me to stop in our tracks, wondering what we were getting into.

Then, just one week later, the mother of one of Judy's boys in school unexpectedly miscarried. Judy and Carol had previously spent a good deal of time together discussing their pregnancies. So knowing of Judy's fall, Carol called shortly after her experience to express concern and to tell Judy some of the symptoms which can signal a miscarriage.

"The most noticeable thing to watch for," said Carol, "is a rapid gain in weight."

At the time Judy thought little about it.

However, not more than seven days later, Judy stepped on the scale.

"Five pounds!" she exclaimed.

Then the following day, hoping the increase to be simply an unpredictable fluctuation which would disappear, Judy again stepped on the scale.

"Another five pounds!" She stared in disbelief.

Following so closely on the heels of Angela's death and Carol's miscarriage, our mind's could not help racing back to Judy's fall. We began to feel the approach of impending doom.

Within a week came Judy's second scheduled doctor appointment. His concern over her ten-pound weight gain and abnormal size prompted the series of tests and X rays. Then his memorable phone call to the store ("Something unusual seems to be going on . . . ") plunged us into the trauma of the pregnancy. First they said the tests indicated a mole. So surgery was scheduled. Then that possibility seemed to lessen. So surgery was cancelled and we were told, "The baby could be dead." All along Dr. Martin tried to reassure us, "Probably everything is fine," but his nervous bedside manner seemed to indicate otherwise.

Our emotions were on a roller coaster ride!

Then came the long week of waiting for Judy's Thursday's appointment to see the specialist who would finally be able to provide some answers. The uncertainty had already been so draining, our prayers by this time were for any *definite* answer. I think we might have been relieved to know once and for all that the baby was dead.

We were learning to thank God in the midst of dark circumstances. It is difficult to really know what it means to "turn it over to God." But during that week, something of that sort seemed to happen inside both Judy and me. There was a "breaking," a letting-go. I was not conscious of our having done anything. I just felt we were a part of something bigger that was happening. Much doubt remained, but we knew God's will would be done. And His will would be for our best. We eagerly anticipated the end of the uncertainty.

Unfortunately it was not to be that easy. Thursday came. The specialist Judy was to see had carefully reviewed all the test and X-ray reports. The first thing he did was to determine if the baby was alive. He hooked up a fetal monitor to listen for the heartbeat.

There was a faint, but distinct heartbeat.

The baby was alive!

His casual comment was, "Well, there's something alive in there." But Judy was bursting with praise to God. He had given us back this little baby!

To us it was as if God had brought a dead baby back to life. Our thoughts immediately went to Abraham and God's promise to him. Though the doctor was not especially overjoyed at hearing the heartbeat, to us it was a special gift from God.

However, additional grim possibilities eventually sifted through the joy into our consciousness. For one thing, the doctor said, there could still be a mole present as well as a live baby. Then he introduced a new word, "polyhydranimous." A polyhydranimous pregnancy is simply one which contains too much water. There can be many reasons for this. But the most frequent cause is a baby having some defect related to its digestive system (no stomach, a throat problem, a deformed mouth which cannot function properly, etc.). This causes the baby to be unable to use the water surrounding it as it normally would. Since the water is unused, it simply builds and builds.

Apparently God did not feel our need then was to have all the uncertainties removed. They continued.

Further tests showed Judy's urine samples to be settling down into the normal range pretty regularly. It began to be fairly clear that the first two tests indicating the presence of a mole were flukes. Whether this was due to a laboratory error or what we never did find out. But Judy's continuing abnormal size and weight (still increasing regularly) and the strong evidence that far too much water existed around the baby seemed to point to the "defective baby" option as the strongest possibility. We dared to hope that the simple explanation for it all was merely that we had misjudged the time of Judy's conception. How nice it would have been if the only problem was that Judy was due in June rather than July.

Thus began another period of waiting. There were no further tests to be done. We just had to see what developed. It had been a difficult several weeks—especially, I think, for Judy. She had the constant physical reminders of our problems and questions with this pregnancy. We dared hope everything would turn out normal, but in the natural it seemed like grasping wildly to do so. Though God had shown the way so clearly in preparation for this baby, this sudden turn of events had jolted us out of thankfulness into a place of constant anxiety. The pregnancy had already seemed like nine months.

We had been thanking God. We knew He was in control and that He had answered our prayers despite our doubts. But that knowledge did not eliminate the burden which hung on us. It would be nice to say, "We praised God, and were victorious . . . !" But it wouldn't be honest. Yes, there was thankfulness in our hearts. But the weight was still there.

How can any person not honestly admit, "We want a normal baby"? We knew the Lord would give us what was for our best. But it remained hard to submit totally and just say to Him, "Be it unto us according to Thy will."

* * *

One of the most severe struggles for Judy throughout this time stemmed from the question ever on her mind, "Is something about my body, my mental attitude, my spiritual make-up in any way responsible for what is happening?" About a year before we had stumbled onto the book *Jesus Wants You Well*,[1] by C. S. Lovett. In reading and applying his principles, many of our attitudes began to change toward our health. We had gone on pseudo health food fads frequently in the past, but sitting down with a bag of doughnuts or a Hostess Twinkie was still not unusual. We had never been thoroughly "converted."

However, after reading Lovett, much of that began to change. He weaves many different strands into his program for total mental, physical, and spiritual health. He does not make it as simple as saying eating health foods will make a difference. But he does say that wise eating, exercising properly, and cultivating your relationship with God through scriptural thinking and acting will profoundly influence all areas of your life. His approach is balanced. It is not a health food book. But he does stress the importance of sound eating and taking vitamins, and offers some very practical and helpful advice. (Through his book we planned out a vitamin program, began to eat brewster's yeast, and started making our own yogurt.) It is not an exercise book. But he does stress that proper exercise must accompany good eating if all-around health is to be maintained. And once again he offers practical help in beginning an exercise program.

His is not a book on spiritual healing. But he discusses at length how it is possible to tap the creative and healing properties that God placed in our bodies through prayer and a balanced mental and physical picture of the wonderful creation that our bodies are.

Jesus Wants You Well caused us to see the importance of our thought patterns in the area of both physical and spiritual health. We thanked God for His timing in incorporating these changes into our daily walk at the time when we were beginning to pray about having a baby. We knew this to be a further example of God's preparation. He stressed to us the necessity of our eating well and taking good care of our bodies for the sake of our future child.

The change in Judy as a result was quickly noticeable. Almost overnight she exhibited a newfound energy. In fact, her improved health was one of the factors which contributed to our decision to have her teach. And with Judy's new vigor came the further realization that God intended to give us a marvelous little child. And through this He was laying the groundwork for that child's health.

Now, however, Satan was attacking us at that very point. He was sowing the seeds of doubt by telling us, "Your bodies aren't so wonderful after all. Just look at all these problems. Your eating and vitamins and thanking God didn't do anything but make it worse."

And we listened! The Bible warns against listening to his suggestions, but when one is under pressure it is difficult to resist.

God, however, proved the stronger. He kept us from total despair, from giving up altogether. We clung tenaciously to our "thanking God, *anyway*" premise. Though our faith was small, God somehow honored it, encouraging us that He was at work. Though unseen in the X rays, tests, or by the doctors, God was *there*. No matter how it turned out, we knew the child was being formed and shaped by the hand of God.

* * *

In the coming weeks and months Dr. Martin tried to reassure us that everything was normal. "We just must have missed the due date." But somehow he didn't convince us. We could hardly help but notice his concern over the extra water (which continued to build—when Judy was eight months along she had gained 45 pounds!) and the puzzled look on his face when examining Judy. He would look at his chart, scratch his head, and then scratch out the due date and write down another. But through the whole process he was questioning and muttering to himself. He was obviously not confident about the change.

This became even more clear when the same ritual would go on again during the next interview, with still another date. We could tell that it just didn't seem right to him.

The intense anxiety of the first few weeks, and the fears of the worst did gradually fade away. Somewhere about five or six months (we were never sure because the due date was so flexible) Judy began to feel movement. That was exciting and drew Judy and me closer together more than any other aspect of the pregnancy. Each little kick ("Oh, there was a good one! Put your hand right here. . . . Oh, there it is! Did you feel it?") somehow assured us that God was making things all right. That special bond which developed between the three of us could not help but allay many of the past fears.

There was still the uncertainty, "Is there something wrong with the baby?" The doctor had admitted it to be a strong possibility. We tried to prepare our hearts as best we could, knowing that the only adequate preparation was simple and thankful hearts. Our prayers were genuine, however doubtful they might have been.

"Lord," we often prayed, "we want your will even though it may be hard for us. We know we're not thankful as we ought to be. Make us thankful. Change our hearts. Let us thank you *always,* not only when the sun is shining."

We also knew that to be given a child with either mental or physical handicaps would be a great blessing. And a great stewardship. We knew God would meet every need and would provide only for our absolute best. Were we to have a handicapped child, then that child would be the *perfect* child for us in every way. No other child could as totally minister to our needs as the child God chose to give us.

It was hard. We couldn't help wanting everything to be fine. But it was impossible for us to pray for a normal child. It had been so up and down, and the lessons of thankfulness so many, that by now all we could say was, "Be it unto us according to your will." It was in His hands.

Judy's deep impression that the Lord had given us back the baby was something which continued to dominate our thoughts. So despite the lingering cloud of questions, we knew that our baby (normal, abnormal, smart, slow, boy, girl) was a gift from God in every way. We didn't know much about that gift as yet. But we knew God had planned it, prepared us for it, conceived and loved it, and given it life, and was now giving it to us. From the moment when the Lord first revealed to Judy, "This child is *yours*, Lord," there was never any further doubt that He was totally in charge.

7

"Goodness!"

As Judy's pregnancy entered its final phases, the silent bond between Judy and me encouraged us in the face of persisting concern. Deep inside we knew we would not fully *know* until the moment the baby was born. We rarely discussed it—just silently sharing the months we had been through together.

Judy continued to get bigger. Even though our July due date was still almost four months away, Judy was one of the largest women in the April natural childbirth class at the hospital, most of whom were due in a matter of weeks. She looked "due" at six months. This occasionally created awkward situations when people would pose the classic comment, "My, are you just about due?"

It isn't easy to hide being pregnant. But in a sense Judy and I wanted nothing more during those last few months than to do just that. We just wanted to wait it out quietly together. But that was impossible. I would daily be asked, "How is Judy? Have you heard anything definite yet?" and Judy would face a barrage of questions also. We did not resent it. We knew our friends cared and were supporting us in prayer. But it had been a wearying six months and we were simply ready for a little rest.

It is difficult to describe our feelings during this time. Judy arrived at school one morning for the teachers' meeting. Noticing that she felt somewhat blue, the others began to pray for her. She could not hold back the tears and had to get up and leave. The only thing that could help was just to be alone for a while. It was not a depression or a deep despair. We were just tired and didn't want to think about it. I felt like Frodo as he approached the mountain, "I am tired, weary.... But I have to go on ..." [1] We found the best tonic was to keep busy so as not to give our lingering doubts a foothold. It helped just to forget everything altogether.

By May Dr. Martin was seeing Judy every two weeks. During her second May visit he was again astounded with her size.

"Incredible!" he exclaimed, months of pent up uncertainties finally bursting through the surface. "There are only two possible reasons you could be so big—a *badly* missed due date ... or twins. I don't care what the first one showed. I'm going to order another X ray!"

Twins! Now *this* was a new wrinkle. "Could it be possible?" she wondered.

In noticeable anticipation Judy stopped by the bookstore on her way to the lab. As she told me of this latest, yet slim, possibility I could sense our hopefulness rising together. Then she left for the lab for "one more" test.

When she was gone my mind relived the past nine months. The accident, the mole, a dead baby, polyhydranimous, digestive disorder, the chart erasings, the theories, the endless perplexities ... " Dare I hope that *today*, within hours, all this uncertainty could be resolved?" I wondered.

The whole thing had been so clouded. How could one simple X ray dissolve it all? But I did hope. How could I help it? "Lord ... " I began, but found no more words to say. What a joy it would be to find that nothing at all had been wrong the whole time. There were just two babies instead of one!

"That would explain everything," I thought. "But could it be? How could it be? The first X ray showed only one baby." Although it made no sense, a terrific hope swelled inside me as I awaited Judy's return. I knew I was foolish to allow myself to get swept away in imagining such a joyful answer. But I could not help myself. My thoughts were not on my customers that afternoon.

Finally the door of the store swung open and in walked Judy. One look at her face told it all! Her eyes were alive and her smile was joyous. She simply nodded her head, flashed up two fingers, and we both laughed.

Such a simple answer!

"But what about the first X ray?" I asked, incredulous yet delighted.

Judy shook her head in mock frustration.

"They took it out of the files, looked again, and then said as if it didn't matter, 'Oh, yes, I suppose there could possibly be another baby there.' Can you believe that?"

No, I couldn't. A misread X ray. What a simple solution to such a seemingly complex dilemma.

But it hardly mattered now. We were rejoicing!

* * *

It was over! The cloud had lifted. We were going to be the parents of twins within two months (the due date remained July 25), although we still could scarcely believe Judy would last that long. We naturally overflowed in thanksgiving to God. But in our quiet moments we sheepishly admitted being somewhat embarrassed. Now that our doubts and anxieties were gone, we were outwardly and unreservedly thankful. We are told to be thankful in *all things*, especially in our trials, and we knew our thankfulness of the last several months had lacked much enthusiasm. But we were learning (and seeing before our very eyes) that God honors His promises in spite of our doubts and limited thanks. Willingness and obedience are the key, not our feelings. We are told to *give thanks*, not to feel thankful.

For the first day in months there was a lightness in our step. I guess maybe we hadn't fully realized the burden of doubt and uncertainty which had settled in upon us until this moment when it was suddenly gone. It was a peaceful day. It was really the first day of the pregnancy when we just were able to sit back and bask in the anticipation of having a child—I mean children! It felt good.

And twins excited us. We had discussed the possibility before, like every expectant couple must, but never seriously (especially after the first X ray). We would joke, "One for you and one for me." As it began to sink in— we liked the idea. We were jubilant. Twins!

"*Twins!* My goodness, do you realize what that means??!!"

It hit us like a brick! How could we lay around soaking up the sun thinking contentedly about having twins when we had but a month or two to get ready for the little people? We had to get to work! Helpful friends brought to our attention what an enormous task lay before us. We had given a lot of thought to having a baby. We knew it would produce many changes and we had pretty much geared ourselves for them. We had somehow convinced ourselves that it wasn't going to be "that hard."

But two! A major change loomed before us, and we knew it. "Would it be twice the work of a single baby? . . . or more?" We didn't know. But we did know it would be hectic and demanding. We flew into high gear!

There was so much we didn't know. "How do you feed two babies? Do you get two of everything? What about breast feeding? Must the husband quit his job? Do you hire a maid? Do you get *any* sleep? How much is it going to cost? Will our new baby room be big enough?" On and on the questions went. So off to the library and to the bookstore we went, hungry to read anything on raising twins by experienced parents.

We devoured what we could find, made lists of things we needed to buy, reorganized the schedules of the store employees so that I would be as free as possible when the time came. It was a determined (but I suppose somewhat futile) effort to get ready for what was in store. It was an eleventh hour attempt, but we enjoyed it. We knew we were desperate and would occasionally start laughing in the idiocy of it all.

We were excited to be having twins. We praised God for the opportunities which lay ahead. What a fruitful God He is! These twins were just one more example of His creativity, His abundance, and the prosperity He showers on His people. We knew there could still be problems with the twins' health. But we did not worry. God had shown himself faithful so completely we knew our prosperity was in Him and His goodness rather than the external appearance of things. No matter what happened, God was behind it all.

How profound was the quote I had learned long ago. Every day I wanted more completely to live its truths:

> The present circumstance, which presses so hard against you, if surrendered to Jesus, is the best shaped tool in the Master's hand to chisel you for eternity. Trust Him then, do not push away the instrument, lest you spoil the work.

There were still questions, however—millions of them. I felt as if I'd been thrown into a class late in the term facing the final exam in a few weeks. There was so much to learn and so little time. We had read a lot on child rearing and felt substantially prepared to handle one baby. This may offer a clue as to why God saw in us a need to have twins—to jolt us out of our self-sufficiency into trusting Him.

The whole area of disciplining twins overwhelmed me at first. The principles had seemed straightforward enough for one. But in trying to coordinate my thoughts together, I found myself asking all kinds of new questions, "What will the influence of disciplining one child be on the other? How will we be able to treat them as individuals? Will it be possible to keep from putting them both in the same mold? Will one feel inferior to the other? How do you deal with that? Will it be possible to keep from showing one more attention than the other? What if one is normal and the other slow?" On and on it went. My mind raced back and forth as I tried to assimilate them all into some order.

Not only these. In addition, I also found myself wondering about money, medical insurance, the store, as well as how twins would affect our marriage and our life. We had been mentally prepared for the adjustment of being "tied down" with one child. But now . . .

"Goodness!"

The size of our family would double overnight. We would be infinitely more restricted than we had been up till now. It was almost more than we had bargained for.

Here was another example of trying to outguess God. He knows our deepest needs and often meets them in ways we could never have foreseen.

The morning after the "news" and the "twin X ray," I awoke early asking the Lord many things. I wandered up to the new baby room I had built (which now looked rather small) and sat down with my Bible.

"Lord, give me some reassurance . . . some guidance . . . some word about all these things flooding my mind," I prayed. I needed some clear direction. I knew I was bogging down in a sea of unanswerable questions.

I flipped through, read sections here and there, and then settled into First Corinthians. In chapters eight and nine I read, "Knowledge can breed conceit, it is love that builds. If anyone thinks that he knows, he really knows nothing yet. But if a man loves, then he is acknowledged by God . . . and if you feel sure you are standing firm, beware! You may fall. God will not allow you to be tested above your powers, but when the test comes he will at the same time provide a way to deal with it."

That was it!

I was guilty of assuming that I had "knowledge" and was standing firm. It had undoubtedly been breeding conceit. God knew exactly what our needs were, and these twins were to be the perfect answer. Through them He would teach us to trust Him where our own insights failed. Possibly we had been prepared for one child. But when you are well prepared, often the need to trust the Lord isn't strong enough. So in His wisdom, God thrust us into a situation where we would be *forced* to trust Him.

But questions and all, I was warmed just to know how dearly Judy and I were going to love our twins. So much thought and prayer and love had been at the root of the decision to have a child in the first place. And it was that love—our love for one another and God's love—which was the foundation for all that would happen in the years to come. God promised in His Word that it would be this love which would build, not our knowledge and our preparation.

The multitude of questions remained. I still sought reasonable answers. I continued to "prepare" as best I could. But the promise of God was that, though important, this preparation was not the key factor in our future success. What mattered most was that we trust God. When the time comes, when a new situation demanding a response arises, *then* He will provide the necessary solution. He would provide the wisdom at the time when it was needed.

8

Ten Pounds of Life

It was amazing how the news of our twins spread among our acquaintances. The appeal of twins is remarkable. Their advent is especially exciting—for everyone. God had blessed us with many people who deeply cared. When the prospects were uncertain they were supporting us in prayer. Many friends we had grown close to through the bookstore had been sharing with Judy and me the doubts, prayers, and thankfulness through the months. And at Judy's baby shower the women of our church prayed for her and the health of the baby. There seemed to be a knitting together of the many people who were prayerfully standing with us.

Now that the outlook was so unusual, I think many people felt that God had specifically answered their prayers.

We were often asked about our reaction to having twins, "Are you scared? How did Judy take it? Are you ready? What did you think?"

All we could answer was, "We are excited. But we realize the tremendous responsibility which suddenly is going to fall on our shoulders." We were to be thrown into a new world overnight. Much of our freedom and mobility would be gone. We'd be tied down like never before. But even so we anticipated this next step. It felt natural to us.

And I think, in a humbling sort of way, Judy and I felt proud too. We knew God had chosen to bless us in this way for a reason, certainly not because of any capabilities we possessed. Having twins was no accident. He had chosen us to bear the responsibility for these two little lives. That filled us with awe. We were eager to discover more about these special gifts He was giving us.

As the time for the births approached, our thinking quite naturally began to turn in the direction of the delivery itself. Child birth is as physically demanding as any other athletic event such as swimming or running. Most women, however, enter the delivery room with no more preparation than an untrained runner entering a national class-mile event. Not only would such a runner be left far behind, he would probably be unable to walk the next day if he had made a hearty effort. For a woman to walk into a hospital to give birth unprepared for what faces her is like being thrown into deep water not knowing how to swim.

Knowing that the birth process was designed by God, Judy and I wanted to study and train and prepare for it however we could. We began a series of natural childbirth classes at the hospital in April. Prior to these classes I had known nothing about the birth process. But through them I gained an appreciation for the beauty of the educated and trained mother giving birth. When we saw a film of an actual birth, something happened inside me. "Lord," I said to myself, "*you created that life!*" It was marvelous. I wanted to be a total part of it with Judy.

There were two main aspects of these classes for me. The most important was simply learning what to expect throughout the various stages of labor. This knowledge builds confidence. I remember when our friends Jim and Joanne Douglas had their baby a year earlier, I wondered, "How did you possibly know when to go to the hospital?" But now after learning the basic pattern of labor and delivery, I was somewhat relaxed about facing it. I knew when the time came we would know what to do.

The second aspect of preparation was in learning what Judy and I could do to ease the pain of labor and make it as short and comfortable as possible. Of course, these two areas are intrinsically bound together. In order to be comfortable during labor, both husband and wife must know what to expect.

The main thrust of the Lamaze method which was taught at our class was in training the mother to relax properly. The husband's role is vital, as a coach rather than spectator. By being well acquainted with the various stages of labor, I was to instruct Judy in performing her "relaxing exercises." By taking the responsibility for noting changes and deciding what procedure to follow, the husband relieves his wife of much added pressure she would otherwise feel. It was my job to time the contractions and then tell Judy what kind of breathing technique to use. When breathing, I would pace her by timing it. All decision-making rests entirely with the husband. The breathing is slow and concentrated when the first contractions come and increases in speed and shortness as the contractions become sharper and closer together. This whole method (neatly summed up in the title of a book which was a great benefit, *Husband Coached Childbirth*, by Bradley) is a well-planned-out program which must be trained and practiced for.

Unprepared expectant mothers have a natural tendency to tense up and become frightened when the pain of contractions first hits them. This is due not only to the pain but also to the uncertainty of what might happen next.

How much better to be trained and ready. The serene wife, under her husband's guidance, maintains self-control and relaxation. Both the training and exercises beforehand and the breathing exercises during labor keep the pain down. The wife is therefore more relaxed. Her body is relaxed, the uterus is relaxed, and the baby can enter the world without the internal tug-of-war which so often is waged. The labor is usually shorter and less painful.

So each evening before bed Judy would faithfully do her "pelvic rocks" and "Kegel muscle exercise," and we would try to practice the breathing rhythm while I did the timing. Toward the end, our days would close with a brief massage of Judy's lower back with a paint roller. We were mentally readying ourselves for those first contractions Judy would feel. They would be our signal to put into practice all we had learned.

Maybe women grow up far more knowledgeable about childbirth than I was. I had never thought of training for this event. Though I had run many races on the track, some for which I had specifically prepared over a year, I had assumed that when one went to the hospital to have a baby, doctors and nurses took over at admittance, and that was that—the baby was born in spite of the mother! So our education in preparation opened up a whole new viewpoint for me. How thrilling it was for me to learn of my part in the process. It would be "our" delivery.

We knew it would probably not happen in typical textbook fashion. There would be the frantic last-minute questions. But it was comforting at least to have a basic idea what to expect. We were anticipating it eagerly. Judy's pregnancy had already seemed like years, and emotionally we were worn out. We were ready to "get on with it."

The time drew shorter. Judy's last days and weeks at school were long and tiring. The stairs up to her classroom seemed higher and steeper every day. When the last day of school finally came on June 14, Judy heaved a sigh of relief.

"Ah, a month and a half to rest!"

I was anxious for Judy to get to bed, unwind, do her exercises, have a chance to do some reading—take a well deserved vacation. However, it was not that easy to slow her down. There was still that final last-minute effort to get ready. Once the babies arrived, they would occupy our time. So we frantically crammed as much as possible into those final weeks.

Then, at last, Judy could relax. It was the third week of June. A month to go.

* * *

During those final weeks I found myself often reflecting on my own parents. It began to dawn on me that they had experienced these very same feelings when I was born. They loved me with the same deep love with which I was loving my yet unborn children. It brought me closer to them in a way I had never felt before.

Following is a letter I wrote to them, trying to express these feelings (it was written prior to the knowledge that we were having twins).

Dear Mom and Dad,

The anticipation of having a baby of our own in a couple of months has really made some changes in me. Ever since we began to think about becoming parents about a year and a half ago, I have found myself thinking more and more about you. For you are *my* parents. And even though in some ways I know you better than any other people in the world, there has always been one area of your lives which I could never actually "enter" and understand. And that is your parenthood. But now I am about to embark upon that adventure myself. It seems that with each passing day, with each kick, and with each reassuring visit to the doctor, I get more excited about that little person inside Judy's body. And I really love that little person, even though I don't know who it is yet. Judy and I know we are going to be good parents because we are really going to love our child. It's going to be fun loving him.

I suppose what makes this really enlightening for me is that I am seeing (maybe for the first time really) how much you two loved, and still love, me. Of course, at this point it is hardly experiential. I am still just anticipating being a father. But now that we have been married three and a half years, I see somewhat more clearly that love which brought you two together. I am seeing that I am a result of your love for each other. And now when I look at old family pictures of you with Cathy, Janet and me, it all becomes so real. You really *love* us! I guess I sometimes think that the way Judy and I love each other is unique. But now I am seeing that you two were every bit as much "in love" as we are. What's more, you must now be loving each other more deeply than ever since your love has now grown for over thirty years. Maybe these feelings are something like learning to honor and reverence age for the great teacher it is. I am coming to respect you for just having gone through many of the things I am going through— and surviving. I know there is much I can learn from you, especially about parenthood. I think one of the greatest preparations for me has been just a thoughtful evaluation of my past. For I have been trained to be a parent for the past twenty-eight years. You both did far more than simply raise me—you trained me. I can hardly tell you how thankful I am to you and to God for that.

Mike

As a child it is natural to take everything for granted. You especially take your parents and the rest of your family for granted. They have always been there and you don't think much about it. There has probably never been a young child who had the slightest inkling of the love and sacrifice which was poured into his life—the love that brought his parents together, the pain his mother felt in bringing him into the world, the *work* of being a parent and caring for a baby, the financial provision made by his father, and the emotional burdens born by both his parents throughout his childhood.

Even though Judy and I still were not parents, our twins had already had much love and prayer. It made me stop to consider the love my parents had for me when I was growing up. I regretted not having realized it fully then. But I was a child, and children just don't have eyes to see it.

How many times I have wished I could go back for a day and be a child again with my current perspective on life and my family. Since I can't do that, I want to be even more aware of these things now.

* * *

Judy's eight-month visit to Dr. Martin was scheduled for Monday, June 23. He again assured us that, notwithstanding Judy's size, we could still be reasonably certain nothing would happen for at least another two or three weeks.

He concluded the visit by saying, "I'm going on vacation for about ten days starting tomorrow. I've made an appointment with Dr. Wright for you tomorrow afternoon. That way in the slight chance you do need to see someone while I'm gone, he'll be familiar with your case."

That unforeseen bit of news was slightly unnerving. In our own minds we didn't see how Judy could possibly last another two weeks. Then on top of everything else our own doctor was going to be gone for what could be the most crucial part of the pregnancy. We just looked at each other and shrugged. What could we do?

When I began to awaken the next morning, the first thing I noticed was that Judy was already wide awake. She said she'd been having some minor contractions since about five o'clock.

I jumped out of bed with a start!

"Stopwatch! Let's see . . . oh, yes, on the table . . . how far apart are they?" I asked through my commotion. "Are they regular? . . . how strong are they?"

"Take it easy," Judy said, trying to calm me down. "I'm pretty sure they're just Braxton-Hicks." (These are irregular contractions which ready the muscles for the onset of labor. Like "warm-up" exercises, they prepare the vital areas for the hard work to come. They are often referred to as false labor and are responsible for sending many an overly anxious couple home from the hospital to wait it out.)

"They don't hurt," she went on. "I can just feel it tightening."

I quizzed her further. Even though they had mostly only been about five minutes apart, they were not painful in the least and had very indistinct beginnings and endings. We naturally wondered if this could be labor but finally concluded that it must indeed be nothing but false labor. We had been so tuned in to the behavior of labor contractions, and these didn't seem to be at all right. But we couldn't tell for sure.

We had one close friend whose labor pains became severe. But when she went to the hospital she had to head back home—false labor! In fact, this had been the warning wherever we turned for knowledgeable advice— "Don't jump the gun!" Going to the hospital too soon seemed to be the earmark of most first-time pregnancies. We lived but a mile from the hospital and weren't about to go too soon.

I went to the store as usual. Judy stayed home trying to force herself to stay in bed. It was hard because she felt good. The tightening "Braxton-Hicks" contractions continued.

Judy's appointment with Dr. Wright was at two o'clock that afternoon. I came home and took her to his office. She told him of the contractions she'd been having and had one for him to observe right during the visit. His response was casual, "I don't think that's anything to worry about. I'm sure it's not labor. Just stay in bed and get as much rest as possible."

Well, that was a relief. "If anyone should know, he should," I said to myself, remembering Dr. Martin's vacation and thinking how ironic it was that he should be gone when things were beginning to happen.

I took Judy home and returned to the store.

When I got home about six o'clock, I could immediately tell that whatever was going on, Braxton-Hicks or the real thing, was beginning to take its toll. The strength of the contractions had been steadily growing along with their regularity. Though Judy insisted there was still no pain, she was clearly beginning to tire some-what. We began to suspect that these contractions might not let up.

"But it's a month early," Judy would insist.

"And this is exactly the pattern of false labor," I would add. "It tries to trick you into going to the hospital too soon."

"And there's no pain," Judy would further add. "Labor is supposed to hurt."

Back and forth we went, trying to convince ourselves that it would soon let up and we could go to bed and worry about it all later. We thought of all kinds of excuses why we should keep waiting. We just kept expecting it to ease up. We were thoroughly convinced that it was false labor. There just hadn't been any of the definite signs.

The evening slowly wore on.

By eight o'clock we were keeping watch. There was slight pain now and the contractions were getting a little more regular. They were still in the neighborhood of five minutes apart, which usually means that hard labor is approaching. We didn't think too much about that, how-ever, since even the faint contractions twelve hours ear-lier had been about that close. We were still in no hurry about leaving. "The hospital is close," we thought. "We'll make it." We wanted to be sure.

We were sitting in bed watching TV, trying to pass the time. After nine, Judy's interest in the program was noticeably flagging. I felt sort of useless sitting there watching Judy in her ordeal and really not able to do anything. The "labor" had been so unofficial that we didn't do all the things we had planned out beforehand. Like my flashing fingers up to instruct her how many breaths to take, or telling her to pick it up or slow it down. I didn't seem to be "comforting and understanding" her as a husband-coach is supposed to do. She just sat quietly and every so often I would notice her breathing intently. But she was totally in control and I hesitated to disturb her. I knew she would let me know when she needed me.

At nine-thirty she was in labor for sure! Now the only question was, "When do we go?" We knew many labors lasted for twelve or fourteen hours. But of course the whole thing depended on when Judy's labor actually began. Were the early contractions Braxton-Hicks which just gradually gave way to labor contractions? Or had Judy actually been in labor for nearly sixteen hours now? Twin labors are usually less severe than others, so it is also possible that labor didn't begin until after I got home that evening. We never did know.

Things then began to move pretty fast.

"We'd better go," I said, getting up to help Judy put on her clothes.

Now that the decision had been made, it seemed to take forever to get ready. Dressing Judy was the hardest part. Every minute or two she would have to stop to breathe and "blow" in short, panting breaths that she had practiced. When we were ready we slowly made our way down the stairs, through the hall, and outside. I poked my head into Mary's room and simply said, "We're on our way," and then we struggled down the steps and into the car, taking one small step at a time and then resting a moment.

Once in the car, we both relaxed a bit. Those last fifteen minutes were a little frightening. We had definitely waited too long. Judy could hardly walk on her way through the house. She had to stop to blow it seemed every minute. But her cool attitude was reassuring. Otherwise we might have unnecessarily panicked, because she was in pain and ready.

We walked (slowly) into the hospital lobby at 10:10. It was obvious what was going on. The receptionist called down to the maternity ward to have someone come down to meet us. We had hobbled about half way there when the nurse reached us. Just as she walked up, a contraction seized Judy. She stopped, grabbed the handrail, and blew frantically.

The nurse asked incredulously, "Are you having the urge to push already?"

Judy simply nodded.

The nurse swung around and called out at the top of her lungs, "*Get me a wheelchair!!*"

Once Judy was in the chair the nurse wheeled her off down the hall at a full run.

Judy was taken into the delivery room as I was half thrown a smock to put on over my jeans and T-shirt. The nurse said as she passed me, "I can't make any promises about your being able to go in there. This is all happening so crazy. But be ready just in case."

I don't think anyone noticed me after that, however. I just walked in behind Judy's gurney and sat down beside her at the head of the delivery table while they got her all fastened into place.

Judy and I looked at each other with a, "Well . . . here we are" expression.

Finally Dr. Wright arrived. He put on his gloves, robe and cap, stepped up to the table and said, "Okay . . . push!"

Almost immediately I could see a tiny little head appear. (I was viewing the delivery in a mirror.)

"Wow!" was all I could mutter in Judy's ear, unable to tear my eyes away from the miracle that was unfolding before me.

Judy relaxed and waited for the next contraction. Then again . . . push! After a few good pushes, a tiny little head emerged, and in another second the doctor was holding a tiny, writhing little baby in his hands—wet and skinny, not exactly a perfect-looking Gerber baby.

"A little boy," the doctor said and Judy and I smiled feebly. I could see she was worn out.

But no rest yet.

The doctor then went after number two. He was breech, so he had to use forceps to twist him into position. It only took three minutes and then out he came, wetting on the doctor's arm on the way out.

"Another boy," said the doctor after a few more minutes. And then added, "Single placenta . . . identical twins!"

The clock showed 10:42. We had been at the hospital only half an hour.

After a few minutes with Judy, I went to phone my parents and Mary at home. Then the news began to find its way to us. Patrick weighed 4 1/2 pounds and was doing fine. Robin weighed 5 3/4 pounds and was having some respiratory problems. I went to look at Patrick after a while, lying there asleep. It was a good feeling. He looked like me.

Looking at Robin, however, was not so joyful. He lay in the intensive care oxygen unit with all kinds of things plugged into him. There was a small team of doctors and nurses taking tests and working on him. We didn't know much of what was happening, but were too emotionally drained to care. We knew it would turn out as God wanted.

I spent the next hour walking between Judy's room and the nursery. I couldn't take my eyes off little Patrick lying there sleeping so peacefully (except for the period when they drew blood over and over from his tiny little heel, squeezing it red, with Patrick screaming—I could hardly stand it.)

It would have been easy to react to the "hospital ways" which seemed so cold, so unnatural. Judy was not even allowed to see or touch the boys until the next morning, and then only briefly. Once you are admitted, it seems as if you are their prisoner, at their mercy. We later had to argue and sign "special" forms to get the boys released. The nurses acted as though they owned the babies under their care and we had no right even to hold them or touch them. I still don't understand that part of it.

But tonight we were too tired and too happy to care. It was over at last.

Walking out of the hospital and driving home in the quietness of the night was strange. I had just become the father of twin boys, our family's size had doubled.

I managed to stay awake just long enough to call Judy's parents, telling them the good news. Then I dropped off to sleep.

At three in the morning I was suddenly awakened by the ring of the phone.

"Mr. Phillips?"

"Yes, it is," I managed sleepily.

"This is Dr. Rosenmeyer at the hospital. I'm working on Robin, and I wanted to fill you in on how the situation stands at this point."

"Oh, yes . . . thank you. . . . " I was coming to.

"Well, he's had some fairly severe breathing problems. We're not quite sure what it is yet, but it seems his lungs just can't quite get functioning properly. Right now it looks as if the chances are about fifty-fifty," Dr. Rosenmeyer concluded.

I listened quietly. I wanted little Robin to be okay, but right now I was too tired to worry. At this time it was relatively easy to give Robin to the Lord because it was obvious there was nothing we could do anyway. He had given Robin life. If He wanted him back again, then like Abraham, we must be willing. Somehow in the haze of my sleep, trusting God with Robin's life was easy. I went back to sleep.

I returned to the hospital the next morning. Judy was tired and sore. Robin was showing some signs of stabilizing. Patrick slept on in his little compartment, disturbed by nothing. They were so tiny.

Of course there were many visitors that day. I spent my time at the store and at the hospital and running back and forth in between. I had to spend one more night alone while the rest of my family slept at the hospital, but Judy came home on Thursday. Because of Patrick's small size and Robin's respiratory problems, both boys had to stay at the hospital longer. When Judy and

I left the hospital on Thursday, the emptiness was even more noticeable. We were leaving just as we had come, except that now we were leaving behind our "family." Already we were attached to them and it was difficult to leave them.

DISCIPLINE

Train a child in the way he should go, and when he is older he will not depart from it.—Prov. 22:6 (author's par.)

Train your children in the loving discipline that the Lord approves.—Eph. 6:4 (author's par.)

The whole meaning of discipline is much closer to "guidance" than to "punishment." [1]

The most significant and joyful fruit which emerges from the love between a man and woman is the children God gives them. "Having" children is but the beginning, however. Once a child is born, if he is to have an eternal relationship with the God who made him, he must be trained and nurtured in the wisdom and love of the Lord. This is an awesome task which faces the new parent. It is a task requiring much thought, much preparation, and much study. God's principles for training children are clear and definite but not always natural. We must seek diligently to discover those principles and then commit ourselves daily to the task of practicing them.

9

Charting Our Course

The one recurring message in every "twin" book we read was this, "At all costs, get some help!" How fortunate for us, therefore, that when the boys were born Judy's parents were in Oregon visiting Mike and Diana and their new little son. They were conveniently able to spend a couple of weeks with us on their way home, and this was a tremendous help. During our first months of parenthood, Judy and I reverted back to our own childhood in one way—being taken care of by our mothers. There is nothing like a birth to bring new grandmothers flocking to the scene. There are many stories told of the new father who is inadvertently shoved into the background by the bossy mother-in-law. But not so in our case. Judy's mom took care of virtually all the chores (meals, washing, housecleaning), thus allowing Judy to relax in bed for several days. And many were the nights when my mother would sit up for most of the night listening for the cry of a hungry little boy, while Judy and I were able to get a few extra hours of sleep. Without our mothers it would have been an absolutely exhausting time.

Though it was hard to leave the boys in the hospital, it turned out to be a blessing in disguise. It allowed us to be gently eased into the tasks which lay before us. Judy came home two days after the delivery; then at five days we brought one baby home, and the other at nine days. So the transition into parenthood came gradually, in manageable chunks. Robin had stabilized by two days and after three days was looking normal in every way. The nurses let us hold him some and Judy began to nurse him.

We went to the hospital three or four times a day to hold both boys and to participate in the feeding times. Patrick was so small and weak that he could nurse very little. We fed him from the bottle. Robin was able to start nursing fairly well so we combined that with a bottle. It was really something, sitting in that hospital holding and feeding our two little boys. All they did was sleep. They looked so peaceful. It was a wonderful experience.

It was hard to leave each time. It seemed as if they still didn't belong to us. But for those few minutes when they were actually resting in our arms, the hospital could have come crashing down all about me and I don't think I'd have heard a thing. Being a father was an experience I was going to like.

The hospital released Robin after five days. I was nervous. No more nurses to hand him back to after the feeding. Now we were on our own for the first time. "What if . . .?" I kept thinking. "Maybe his breathing problem would flare up. Then what . . .?" It was somewhat frightening.

But everything went fine. We put him in his cradle in our bedroom and began the never-ending process of feeding him every two or three hours round the clock. Somehow I was surprised to find how difficult it was to get any significant sleep those first few nights. It should have been obvious that it would be like that. I don't know why it took me by surprise. But it did. That cry in the night was coming long before I was ready for it. I'm glad we were able to get used to one at a time.

I'm sure every new parent remembers the first night with the baby. We were uneasy throughout the whole first night with Robin. His breathing had such an irregular and jerky sound that it became the first thing we strained our ears for whenever a moment of wakefulness would come upon us. I suppose we half expected him to stop breathing suddenly and die. But the first morning arrived on schedule and after that our nervousness subsided.

We were sad having to leave Patrick "alone" in the hospital. (He had to reach five pounds before they'd release him—another hospital "regulation.") But by the time he came home at nine days, Robin was nursing somewhat regularly and had settled into a routine of sorts. I still recall vividly those first few days. All I wanted to do when I came home from the store was to pick up Robin and lay back on the bed holding him to my chest. What a feeling! He just slept and slept, and it was so peaceful.

The biggest difficulty (other than obtaining enough of that precious commodity—sleep!) of the first months centered around our feeding of the boys. Because of our natural foods background and the importance to us of providing these babies with every possible nutritional advantage, Judy had planned to nurse since before even being pregnant.

But long before our babies were born we decided we would not be strongly pro or con regarding nursing. Situations vary and so do ways of dealing with them. We knew that breastfeeding vs. bottle feeding was not really a key issue. What mattered was the attitude in a woman's heart toward her child. God is big enough to use a multitude of different methods to handle things that come up. This is true in all aspects of life. Why should nursing be any different?

So I determined to put no pressure on Judy one way or another. She wanted to nurse but wasn't going to be hung up about it if she couldn't—especially once we learned we were having twins. She knew that trying to nurse two babies would be at least three times the effort of nursing one. So she approached it very calmly.

While the boys were still at the hospital, Judy tried to nurse them with no success at all. They were so tiny and weak. Nursing required such an effort that poor Patrick would fall asleep in the process. They seemed to do all right using the hospital bottles, though.

When Robin came home, after a few days he began to get the hang of it and by about two weeks was nursing fairly consistently. Patrick was pretty used to the bottle by the time he came home and was not too interested in nursing for quite some time. Judy kept at it, though, and after about a month he was handling it well too.

All of the information she read about nursing twins said, "You can, you can, you can!" However, she was to find that "you'll have more than enough milk" was another "pat answer" she had to work around. There were many times when Judy just plain didn't have enough milk for the two of them. It was just as simple as that. All women are not made the same.

So we gave them both at least one bottle a day from the very beginning. Our reasons were several. First of all we wanted the option available to go either way. With twins you are forced to cut a lot of corners, and we wanted to make sure that our boys were equally comfortable either way. Secondly, Judy never did have enough milk to fully feed them both all they needed. Sometime one of the boys would nurse for fifteen or twenty minutes and we would then carefully and precisely weigh him, comparing the weight to a reading made before the feeding, to see if he was getting what he needed. "Not even an ounce!" we would exclaim in unbelief. No wonder he would be hungry in another hour. Thirdly, bottle feeding enabled me to be more a part of the process and relieved some of Judy's burden. A complete feeding would sometimes take over an hour when both boys nursed, which is really draining when the whole process begins again in another two hours.

After about a month the boys settled into a fairly consistent pattern of eating. Much advice says that "four-hour schedules" should be followed rigidly as soon as possible.

Again, others say it just won't work the same for all babies. We tried it and went crazy the first time trying to hold them off until four hours! We quickly decided that we had to just "feel our way" and not try to conform to everything we read.

The nursing went well enough. But I'm convinced one of the reasons was Judy's adaptability. We realized we had to "chart our own course" and so we experimented with different methods, schedules, etc., until we found a system that was right for Judy and for the boys. There is no other way. You simply must be open to a wide range of suggestions and ways to go about things. Flexibility is important. Raising an infant is difficult. There are a lot of questions, most of which do not have nice, neat, compact answers.

A further aspect of nursing which is rarely discussed by pro-breastfeeding advocates is the tremendous drain to your system. It does tax your body! After four or five months Judy was so tired from her twenty-four-hour-a-day routine, we wondered if nursing might be taxing her more than we knew. She talked to a friend who said, "Practically the minute I stopped nursing, my energy was doubled."

So at five months she decided to ease away from nursing. And her physical response was the same. Within weeks she was full of energy again and more mentally able to approach each new day with enthusiasm. I'm glad Judy nursed our boys, but I'm equally glad she stopped when she did. Being a mother is demanding enough without adding to the burden of it unnecessarily. If Judy does not nurse our next child, I'll appreciate her nonetheless. For I know the important thing is her godly characteristics as a woman and mother. That is what I appreciate in her. As she transmits those characteristics to our children, they will be nurtured in love. To nurse or not to nurse, that is not the question. The question is to be comfortable and at peace in whatever manner

God directs you to follow.*

There were a host of other areas where "pat answers" were to cause us frustration—until we finally learned that convenient solutions to complex problems are very few. Diaper rash was another example. Both Patrick and Robin had severe red rashes, sometimes blistering and peeling. We tried all the formulas—talcum powder, corn starch, ointments by the truckload, disposable diapers, cloth diapers, leaving off the plastic pants, rinsing diapers in vinegar during each wash, leaving off the diapers altogether, laying them exposed in the sun, etc. We even tried a home remedy of stove browned white flour instead of powder. The doctor could offer no help. With no apparent concern, he blithely suggested the same things we'd been using for months. It went on for months. Nothing helped.

Then when Judy was having the boys checked at the Health Department, the public health nurse noticed a rash behind their ears and in the folds of their necks.

"Why, they've got eczema," she said.

She prescribed a simple prescription and within days the diaper rash was gone.

This time the answer itself was simple, but its discovery took months. We were discovering that with children, every situation is made complex by the thousand individualities which distinguish it from a similar situation with another child. Doctors are sometimes just as fully at a loss as the poor parents.

At about four months Patrick began to show some frightening signs. Late in the day or sometimes right after a feeding, he would start to cry in a totally new way. It was awful! It was clearly due to one thing only—pain!! But we had no idea what to do. Usually it would subside after two or three hours. We took him to the

---

* For a more complete look at some of the pros and cons of nursing, as well as some of the frustrations which can arise from them, see Appendix 1 at the back of the book.

doctor, but he could tell us nothing!

Then we began to notice that his crying would be associated with a lump in his groin.

"A hernia," we thought.

But when we mentioned it to the doctor at the next visit, he did not seem alarmed.

One day it got so bad we took him to the emergency room at the hospital, but again the doctor was unable to tell us anything.

Finally we decided that the doctor would have to see Patrick right at the peak of his intense crying. So when the next one hit, we called Dr. Martin, got him out of bed, and said we were going to the hospital. But even then, with the lump bulging right before all of us, his comment was, "I just can't tell for sure . . . but we'd better have someone else take a look at it."

The specialist confirmed that Patrick did, indeed, have a fairly serious double hernia. He was operated on the next week. (The day after Patrick's surgery, Robin suddenly "caught" his symptoms and eventually also had the same operation.)

How nice it would have been for the doctor to have been able to take out his little reference book, flip to the page on "crying," and read, "Crying is caused by . . . To relieve the situation, do this. . . . "

But it just isn't that easy with children. Even doctors are often experimenting with different answers themselves. Expecting simple solutions to all the situations faced by new parents leads only to frustration.

In addition to the ever helpful Dr. Spock, two other books we often referred to were *Dr. Turtle's Babies* and *Let's Have Healthy Children*. But even these authorities only provide direction, not always answers. Dr. Spock says, "If your baby has a cold during his first year, the chances are that it will be mild . . . He is not likely to have a fever." [2] Dr. Martin told us the same thing. "Babies rarely get colds under a year."

Patrick was born with a cold, I think. We spent several months syringing out his nose. (He hated it!) It was complete with all the "stuff" so generously produced by a stuffy nose, "stuff" which was not even supposed to exist in a child his age.

Both Robin and Patrick had high fevers at about seven months. Robin's reached 104°. However, just to keep the record straight, Dr. Spock was extremely helpful here. By following his recommendations for a fever, we brought it down almost immediately.

At nine months again, both the boys had severe colds, complete with a chest cough, sneezing, lack of sleep, wheezing, red noses, mucous, and discomfort. "No colds under a year," but they lasted a week and a half, whatever they were.

How to relieve diarrhea also provided one of those "comical" situations where a straight answer seemed difficult to find. After their fevers, the boys had persistent diarrhea which we tried to get rid of.

In her book Adelle Davis had said that the best way to get rid of diarrhea was to give whole milk, yogurt, and lots of solid food.

Then we went to Dr. Spock only to read just the opposite—skimmed milk and no solids.

> If he is taking solids, too, omit them until . . . the diarrhea is cured . . . diluted skimmed milk [is even better] . . . omit all solids . . . Skimmed milk . . . is often prescribed for diarrhea, because milk is easier to digest when there is no cream in it.[3]

Well, what do we do now? One says whole milk, solids, and yogurt. The other says skim milk, no cream, no solids. Two exactly opposing solutions by two leading authorities! Don't get me wrong. We have pored over both these great books and have received *much* help from them. But again, the key is charting your own course. Every baby is unique.

(After trying skim milk, we started the boys back

on yogurt—which they had been off during their fevers. Less than twenty-four hours after the yogurt began, they were back to normal.)

10

Adjustments and Readjustments

Children bring enormous changes into a marriage. Usually one of two things begin to happen between a man and woman after the arrival of their first child. Either they are drawn together into a closer unity and love than ever before or a tiny rift develops between them which deepens and widens in later years. Being a Christian is no automatic guarantee this gap will not develop. It happens even in the best of marriages, often gaining a foothold before it is even noticed. Indeed, awesome as these marital changes can be, they take place so slowly they often go unnoticed until long after they began.

Since the boys were born the struggle to remain close increased for Judy and me. We have not always succeeded by any means and are far from having that "sure" method which keeps walls from developing between us. It takes a decided effort to stay close. It is just no good saying "trust the Lord, and it will all be okay." It takes some down-to-earth unselfishness on both sides to keep from occasionally losing sight of the love which brought you together.

Usually by the time children first come along a husband is reaching the point in his career where some major decisions are being called for. These decisions affect the course of his entire future. A tremendous commitment is usually required of men at this point in their lives. And no matter what sort of job a man has, there is something inside him which desires to achieve, to be successful. This need not be a monetary goal at all. His goal may be to reach the world for Christ. But that vision consumes such a man with the same totality as the drive to be a millionaire does a worldly executive. God has built into man this urge, this drive, this capacity to produce, this excitement over the work God has given him to do. It need not be an ego-related thing at all. Though it can, of course, be perverted, this basic drive is God-given. The vision which keeps a man up nights is the same vision which compelled Paul to travel over half the world, "on fire" to tell people about Jesus.

So when a baby suddenly enters the picture, the enthusiastic young man is faced with a new situation—one for which he may not have bargained. All at once his wife is no longer his constant companion, the sounding board for his new ideas. No longer does their home revolve around him, his job, his homecoming, his vacation. Instead, his wife now has a full-time commitment of her own—usually more demanding than even his job.

As he comes home at night he realizes that he no longer lives in the same world as is now consuming his wife. She no longer meets him for lunch or calls him during the day or greets him at the door with a kiss. Rather than, "How was your day, dear?" he is handed a bottle or a baby to change while she frantically tries to throw some dinner together. There are toys on the floor, dishes in the kitchen, and beds unmade.

Of course, this man loves his wife and his new little child. He has probably been anxious to get home to be with his wife and baby and is only too glad to help. He wants to be a part of the process too. But the subtle changes taking place are already visible. Eventually the newness of being a father will wear down and the pressures of the job will again begin to take precedence. Unless they both watch what is happening, sometime in the first year or two following the birth of their first child, a rift will slowly begin to develop between them. Unless a man is well prepared for these changes ahead of time, he will tend to close himself off from his wife and children. A tension can then develop which will ultimately be directed toward his wife and children. And if a woman is not careful, she can begin to harbor a bitterness toward her husband when she realizes that other things are very important to him too—things that are outside her life.

A man's priorities must be clearly defined ahead of time. If his family is to take priority over his career, then he must face that decision squarely before any frustration develops.

"Pat" answers are just no good here. These issues are real. I have been blessed with a job that enables me to leave it occasionally when necessary. When the boys were born I spent a good deal of time at home helping out. I loved it! I wanted to be part "mother." And throughout their first months of life I probably helped out more than the average husband would be able to. Whenever possible, I would come home to help with the afternoon feedings. Not only was it enjoyable for me, it also enabled Judy to take a nap or go shopping. I knew she needed me as much as I could possibly give.

But there were still a host of other things that continued to demand my attention. For Judy the primary involvement of her life was our home and the boys. There were not a lot of outside interests vying for her attention. Not so for me. Many business pressures and decisions eventually began to resurface, and I began to feel drawn in several directions at once. Our store was at a crucial stage. We were considering several aspects of rather serious expansion which would involve years of commitment, many thousands of dollars, and new personnel. Planning and thinking through these changes, considering what direction our business was to move in future years, was draining, and I admit it was difficult to come home and have to shift gears immediately.

Judy was marvelous. She put little pressure on me. But I realized she was also under great stress herself and needed me to encourage and support her every bit as much as I needed her to understand my emotional needs. I wanted to help her and tried to understand and ease her burden whenever I could. But it was not always easy. Some evenings all I could do was "plop down" in my chair. I would do it knowing full well there were things I could be doing to help. I offer no solutions. I just say this common dilemma was something we experienced too. I continue to feel this pull in many directions and it is no easy problem to sort out.

Sometimes I fall into the trap of thinking, "If I just give the store my all for the next five years, then when the boys are old enough to go places, read, talk with me, etc., *then* I'll spend more time with them. *Then* we'll be in sound enough financial shape so that I won't have to spend fifty or more hours a week at the store. *Then* I'll be able to give them more of myself."

But that is no good. It is a dangerous attitude which traps many fathers. I understand it, for it has a certain appeal as the way out of the immediate problem. I find myself toying with the idea occasionally until I suddenly wake up to its deceit. Twenty years later, the man who followed that suggestion, probably very wealthy and successful, one day realizes that his children are grown and their very lives have passed him by

"Where did the years go?" he asks himself.

But it is too late. They are gone forever. For the man who continually says, "Tomorrow I'll do better," tomorrow never comes. Tomorrow the little baby won't want to be held, the toddler won't be scampering into your lap, the five-year-old won't be asking you to read him a story, the ten-year-old won't be asking you to play ball, the teenager won't be asking your counsel about school and girls and making the team. By the time "tomorrow" comes, the young man who only "yesterday" was your little baby will have made many of his major decisions in life and will have gone his way.

Listen to the lyrics of the song, "The Cat's in the Cradle."

My child arrived just the other day;
he came to the world in the usual way.
But there were planes to catch and bills to pay;
he learned to walk while I was away.
And he was talkin' 'fore I knew it,
and as he grew he'd say, "I'm gonna be like you, Dad,
you know I'm gonna be like you."

And the cat's in the cradle and the silver spoon,
little boy blue and the man in the moon.
"When you comin' home, Dad?"
"I don't know when, but we'll get together then;
you know we'll have a good time then."

My son turned ten just the other day;
he said, "Thanks for the ball, Dad; come on, let's play.
Can you teach me to throw?"
I said, "Not today. I got a lot to do."
He said, "That's okay."
And he, he walked away, but his smile never dimmed,
it said, "I'm gonna be like him, yeah,
you know, I'm gonna be like him."

Well, he came from college just the other day;
so much like a man I just had to say,
"Son, I'm proud of you; can you sit for a while?"
He shook his head and he said with a smile,
"What I'd really like, Dad, is to borrow the car keys;
see you later; can I have them please?"

I've long since retired, my son's moved away;
I called him up just the other day.
I said, "I'd like to see you if you don't mind."
He said, "I'd love to, Dad, if I can find the time.
You see, my new job's a hassle and the kids have the
flu,

but it's sure nice talkin' to you, Dad;
it's been sure nice talkin' to you."
And as I hung up the phone, it occurred to me,
he'd grown up just like me,
my boy was just like me.

And the cat's in the cradle and the silver spoon,
little boy blue and the man in the moon.
"When you comin' home, Son?"
"I don't know when, but we'll get together then, Dad,
we're gonna have a good time . . . then." *

As clear and obvious as this deceitful line of thinking is, I have found myself falling for it. "Just around the corner is the break I need. *Then* . . . I'll be free to give myself."

But it will never happen. It is an illusive dream. If you don't give yourself now, you never will.

Though it is hard, this is why I try not to ever ignore one of my boys. I emphasize "try." I am no ideal father. It is a daily struggle for me to give my "self" to these boys, though I love them as I've loved few things in my life. If I am busy and Patrick is crying and needs some attention, I try to make myself go to him *now*. I can't wait even five minutes, even if what I am doing is important and "I've just got another five minutes and I'll be done!"

That five minutes will never come again. I must act now. How awful to have little Patrick grow up thinking, "I was always just five minutes too late for my father. Something else always beat me to him." By waiting I can easily drift into a pattern of waiting, ignoring, becoming calloused to his cries. Suddenly Patrick will be a man, "waiting" for his father to care.

So I determine to be available *now*. I don't always succeed. But I know this is what I must do. One day when the boys were about nine months old, Judy was changing Robin in the washroom. I came walking through

---

on my way to the garage. As he heard my steps, Robin's face lit up in a huge smile. I never saw it because I was quickly gone. Judy just saw the smile slowly fade away. I hadn't noticed and hadn't given him anything. It would have been so easy to respond to that smile, to squeeze him or kiss him or say his name. He needs that reciprocal love. As parents we are the supreme light of their lives for several years. Nothing we do goes unnoticed by them. But when we ignore them, the "smile will slowly fade away." Let that not become the pattern of a child's early years—a "fading smile."

When Patrick was first crawling, his only target was a lap, a foot, a leg, an arm. While Robin could interest himself in a toy, a cord, a table leg, Patrick's sole ambition was to climb onto some piece of humanity, any piece. I could see in his eyes a look of supreme purpose. I've never seen such intensity. He gasped, struggled, squirmed, and threw himself *completely* into the process of getting into that lap. There was fire in his eyes.

To us it seems so small. We've got things to do. I must get ready for work, Judy has to fix the bottles, there's a day to face and work to do. But to Patrick, there was *only one thing*—getting into that lap! In his world, that was as great a struggle as my dad's living through the Great Depression. I cannot shrug off such an effort just because I've "got things to do." It's hard to cater to it every time. Yet at Patrick's age, how we respond to his question, "Do you love me? I want to be in your lap," sets the pattern for later years. In their tiny world everything is important. We must get into their world at every level if we are going to be parents who teach their children about "todays" rather than "tomorrows." Today it is a lap, tomorrow it may be looking at a bug together, and next it may be going to watch him in the school band. But we must never ignore the immediately important thing to him, no matter how insignificant it seems to us.

I do not always succeed. But this is what I must

aim for. Every new parent must clearly think out these things ahead of time. You must be aware of your priorities and know beyond any doubt that your family is on top. Tiny things form a pattern from which it is difficult to escape later. You must learn to set things aside which you otherwise might do. You must recognize the value of a "project" when compared to the life of your child. What comparison is there!? But how easy it is to forget when the baby has been crying for half an hour and you've "just got to get this little project finished." So you tune him out.

*   *   *

If there have been adjustments and changes for the new father, imagine what the new mother has gone through! She has usually been able to arrange her own time, but suddenly she has to wait on a crying and insistent little baby for fifteen or twenty hours a day. There are no breaks, no vacations, no days off—no recess! And when the little guy does finally fall asleep, she needs the time just to catch up on her own sleep, the wash, the dishes, the housework, and fix dinner besides. A new mother's list is long and never seems to diminish.

Then when evening comes she also has a tired husband. She's got to try to sympathize with his problems on the job, his frustrations, his aspirations, his ambitions. As if her new little son or daughter doesn't give her enough to worry about without also having to be wife, mother, partner, lover, friend, and counselor to her husband. Hers is a demanding and wearying task. Is it any wonder that a new mother experiences frustration and depression if her husband comes home and sits down in front of the TV for the evening, leaving her to clean up after dinner, fold the clothes, fix tomorrow's bottles, and make the bed before they retire for the night? It would be easy for a woman in such a situation to resent her husband very quickly.

Even in our situation, where I have made what efforts I can in helping Judy, there are times when I suddenly "see," and think to myself, "Here I am sitting in front of the TV while Judy (who has been on the go since 6:30 this morning) is frantically trying to finish out the day, keeping her 'TTD' list no longer than it was at the start of the day." There are times when her eyes fill with tears just because she hasn't been able to find time to squeeze in a shower for five days. And I am sometimes no help at all. It is easy to go on working on my own little projects without giving any regular and significant help. Can I blame her for occasionally becoming frustrated with me? She has every right to.

In his book dealing with the sources of depression among women (*What Wives Wish Their Husbands Knew About Women*), Dr. Dobson lists fatigue and time pressure as the highest frustrations for women. He describes the "running" of the mother of young children.

> Not only is she rushed from morning to night, but she experiences an unusual kind of emotional stress as well. Youngsters between two and five years of age have an uncanny ability to unravel an adult nervous system. Maybe it is listening to the constant diarrhea of words that wears Mom down to utter exhaustion. Hasn't every mother in the world had the following "conversation" with her child at least a million times?
>
> > "Can I have a cookie, Mom? Huh, Mom? Can I? Can I have one, Mom? Why can't I have one? Huh? Huh, Mom? Can I? Mom? Mom, can I? Can I have a cookie now? . . ."
>
> . . . there is nothing on the globe to parallel the shortage of energy in a young mother between 6:00 and 9:00 p.m.! The dinner is over and the dishes are stacked. She is already tired, but now she has to get the troops in bed. She gives them their baths and pins on the diapers and brushes their teeth and puts on the pajamas and reads a story and says the prayers and brings them seven glasses of water. These tasks would not be so difficult if the children wanted to go to bed. They most certainly do not, however, and develop extremely clever techniques for resistance and postponement. It is a pretty dumb kid who can't extend this ten-minute

process into an hour long tug-of-war. And when it's finished and Mom staggers through the nursery door and
leans against the wall, she is then supposed to shift gears
and greet her romantic lover in her own bedroom. Fat
chance! [1]

The most deadly aspect of fatigue and time pressure
faced by both men and women trying to cope with the
changes of marriage, parenthood, and careers is how
their children are affected. If these pressures drive a
wedge between husband and wife, the effects on their
children are devastating. Again I quote from Dr. Dobson:

Dad is holding down three jobs and he huffs and
puffs to keep up with it all. Mom never has a free
minute, either. Tomorrow night, for example, she is
having eight guests for dinner and she only has this
one evening to clean the house, go to the market, arrange the flowers for the centerpiece, and put the hem
in the dress she will wear. Her "to do" list is three
pages long and she already has a splitting headache
from it all. She opens a can of "Spaghetti-Os" for the
kids' supper and hopes the troops will stay out of her
hair. About 7 p.m., little Larry tracks down his per-
spiring mother and says, "Look what I just drawed,
Mom." She glances downward and says, "Uh huh,"
obviously thinking about something else.

Ten minutes later, Larry asks her to get him some
juice. She complies but resents his intrusion. She is behind schedule and her tension is mounting. Five minutes
later he interrupts again, this time wanting her to reach
a toy that sits on the top shelf of the closet. She stands
looking down at him for a moment and then hurries
down the hall to meet his demand, mumbling as she
goes. But as she passes his bedroom door, she notices
that he has spread his toys all over the floor and made
a mess with the glue. Mom explodes. She screams and
threatens and shakes little Larry till his teeth rattle.

Does this drama sound familiar? It should, for
"routine panic" is becoming an American way of life. . . .
There was a time when a man didn't fret if he missed
a stagecoach; he'd just catch it next month. Now if a

fellow misses a section of a revolving door he's thrown into despair! But guess who is the inevitable loser from this breathless lifestyle? It's the little guy who is leaning against the wall with his hands in the pocket of his blue jeans. He misses his father during the long day and tags around after him at night, saying, "Play ball, Dad!" But Dad is pooped. Besides, he has a briefcase full of work to be done. Mom had promised to take him to the park this afternoon but then she had to go to that Women's Auxiliary meeting at the last minute. The lad gets the message—his folks are busy again. So he drifts into the family room and watches two hours of pointless cartoons and reruns on television.

Children just don't fit into a "to do" list very well. It takes time to introduce them to good books—it takes time to fly kites and play punch ball and put together jigsaw puzzles. It takes time to listen once more to the skinned-knee episode and talk about the bird with the broken wing. These are the building blocks of self-esteem, held together with the mortar of love.[2]

This is marriage. This is parenthood. This is family relationships. In many ways it is certainly not what Judy and I expected, and without major efforts from both of us (toward each other and toward our children), I can see that we could enclose ourselves in our own private worlds. Our prayer must be, "Lord, make us willing to give."

* * *

So husbands, wives, parents—you have two choices. You can take things as they come with little foresight or planning and run the risk of allowing the day's "urgencies" to dictate the pattern your life follows. Or you can carefully think out your priorities and plan a strategy for building them into your daily life. The "tyranny of the urgent" will indeed control you unless you decide with determination to place the "important" above the "urgent." The following suggestions I make to husbands and wives are based on the necessities Judy and I have observed in our own marriage. They are hard to do. There is no fairness about them. If you want to react, "But why do I have to do it all?" then you might as well not even read them. If you're not to the point where you're willing to pay any price to keep a rift from developing between you and your husband or wife, then you will probably not make the effort anyway.

But if, on the other hand, you *do* see many of these potential danger signs developing in your marriage and between you and your children, then you do have the power to turn your family around and make it the most exciting experience ever to come along. Just remember, *you* are responsible all the way, one hundred percent, for any changes that are going to come about. Do *not* expect your husband or wife to do "their fair share." Either partner, giving all to the other, can put life back into the family. But two partners, each willing to give fifty percent if the other will give his, will get nowhere. This is one case where two halves do *not* make a whole.

So to the wives I offer this counsel. *Make your husband king!* Even if you have three sets of twins all under age four (Don't laugh! It has happened), you must make an all-out effort to understand the pressures that crowd in on your husband when he is away from home. You've got to try to share that life with him—as much as you did before you had children. The methods will, of course, be vastly different. But your husband will know that you are interested and that you care. His home must still be the place where he can unburden and be refreshed. God has given him a task to do. To him it is the greatest calling he could be asked to follow. Without your understanding and support and encouragement, he will not be able to mount to the tasks which face him. He will fail without you. No matter what it may "appear" to you sometimes, yours is the only love and understanding he *really* cares about. You must have faith in him. There will be many times when your husband feels he is standing all alone. Without you there beside him, he *will* be standing alone. So make his life your number-one concern, even above your children. God gave you to him for this purpose.

Naturally the children will change the ease of your being a part of your husband's life. And they will change the ways you will be a part of his life. But they change nothing else. If anything they increase the importance of "loving and honoring him." You must raise your children from the day they are born to understand by the way you act that "Daddy is *king!*" Don't expect him to change and now focus his entire energy on you and the children. It's got to be you that focus on him.

When he comes home, greet him warmly. Share his work with him. Don't unleash your day of burdens the moment he walks in the door. Make his home a place where he can relax, feel comfortable, do whatever he pleases. Let him watch TV, putter around in the yard or garage, or read a book without having to feel guilty. Never convey by your "silent attitude" that "without me this house would fall apart." If that thought is in your mind, believe me, your husband will know it! And nothing will kill his motivation to give you a hand with the dishes after dinner sooner than your *expecting* it from him.

Make home the most enjoyable place on earth for your husband. Make him king and make your home his castle. It doesn't have to be spotless. He understands that kids make a house a mess in five minutes. It is your attitude, your love, your appreciation of him that will make it his favorite place to be. Don't pressure him. If he begins to find home an unpleasant place, he will simply find an appropriate substitute. But if you love him with ceaseless giving, your husband will "come alive" overnight. That may sound "one-sided," a big order for the mother of small children, but it is nothing more than what Jesus commanded of us, "If anyone would be first, he must be last of all and *servant* of all." Your marriage will be exciting each day in new ways, and your children will grow up knowing what love means.

They have seen it at work! You women have the power to make that happen in *your* marriage!

Husbands, your calling is to make your wife queen. But hers is not a royalty of thrones, robes and crowns. Hers is a royalty whose founder was a king because He submitted to a cruel death. Hers is the royalty of Jesus, the royalty of servanthood. For most of her married life, your wife will serve you. She cooks, cleans, sews for you. She raises your children. She gives her life for them because of her love for you and them. Hers is a never-ending life of service. And she does it *joyfully*! God planted within the heart of your wife a capacity to love and serve, which is largely unknown to most men.

You must never allow yourself to forget that your wife is going through more significant changes as a mother than you will probably ever face in your life. Now that there are children in the home, her workload is undoubtedly heavier than yours and the time demanded of her is far greater. No longer can the fact that you are the "bread winner" get you off the hook from helping around the house. You spend probably no more than forty or fifty hours a week at your job. You wife puts in seventy and eighty hours a week minimum. Without your help she will simply crack—physically as well as emotionally. In addition to the sheer exhaustion of her pace and workload is the frustration which cannot help but enter your relationship if the burden of the children is all upon her.

They are your children. Learn to joyfully spend time with them. Take care of them while your wife goes shopping. Give her the chance to sleep in occasionally, while you get them up and take care of the morning "chores." Help her feed them, clothe them, be an integral part of the raising of your children. Your effectiveness in disciplining them later will be a direct result of the time you give them in their early years. How can you discipline them and love them if you don't spend enough time getting to know them?

When you come home at night and when you are home on weekends or for vacations, pitch in with your wife. Share her life with her. Let her know you understand and appreciate the sacrifices she makes for you and for the home and for the children. Give her a hand with the work. One of the most important things for your wife is to know that you are "with her." It encourages her to have your support.

"I realize what a load you have to carry. I think you do it nobly. Let me know if there's *anything* I can do to help." Those words are worth more to a woman than any gift you could give her.

One of the most important issues I have had to come to grips with is the realization that since our boys were born Judy does not have the outside opportunities to relate with people that I do. I have hundreds of varied contacts each day, while she faces the exact same routine *every* day. For her it is an exciting event to get to go outside with the boys for fifteen minutes. An hour "off" at the store, catching up on her bookkeeping, is a delight! I have to remind myself constantly that Judy needs opportunities to "get away" and she needs my sensitive understanding. She needs to know that I understand these frustrations she faces. And I must work at staying sensitive to them. It is easy to forget. Our lives are lived in different arenas. I must ever remind myself that her arena is isolated and needs my presence often.

A wife needs constant upbuilding. Children are draining. They drain the emotions as well as the body. But for a woman, the two are related. When a woman feels hot and sweaty and hurried, her emotions suffer. She can become depressed over things that may seem small to her husband. But they are not small! They seem small to us because they are different from things we face. But for your wife, they are *huge*! She needs to know that you love her. She needs to know that she is attractive to you. Build up your wife. Compliment her. Love her. Enjoy her. Make sure your wife knows she is just as pleasing to you as the day you married her. (She should be even more so!) The only way a woman can be refilled with the spirit and enthusiasm which young children tap is by a loving husband who encourages and upbuilds her at every opportunity. Raising a family demands sacrifices. Do not expect your wife to make them all.

Husbands and wives, both, remember—don't keep track of your mate. These last pages were written to give you each specific ways to love your partner, not to provide a list for you to evaluate how the other is doing. Do your part and let God take care of your partner.

Finally, to the woman I offer these brief quotes from *The Total Woman:*

> You have the power to lift your family spirit or bring it down to rock bottom. The atmosphere in your home is set by you. If you're cheery tonight, chances are your husband and children will also be cheery.[3]

> You are the one person your husband needs to make him feel special. ... He needs your admiration. He needs it to live. Without it all his motivation is gone.[4]

> It is only when a woman surrenders her life to her husband, reveres and worships him, and is willing to serve him, that she becomes really beautiful to him.[5]

To the man I offer but this simple injunction from the 31st chapter of Proverbs:

> Rise up and call your wife blessed!

If you can do this every day, you will have a happy marriage and you will be a man fulfilling the destiny to which God called him. Find ever new ways to encourage and bless her. Lavish your love upon her. Lose no opportunity to bless and praise her for the woman and wife she is. She is your *queen*! Let not a day pass that she is not reminded of this!

11

Training—A Many-Faceted Responsibility

As already recounted, years earlier Judy and I had been forced to think through authority in all of its varied aspects to get our marriage back on the track. This thinking later led us into the area of discipline, especially when Judy faced a classroom of active young boys. But once we had our own boys, our thoughts moved on to what I would term child "training," of which discipline is only one part. We found ourselves concerned with building many things into the lives of our children—foundations for deep and healthy relationships, respect for authority, self-esteem, creativity, love, trust, faith in God, imagination, and humility. An awesome undertaking to say the least! We knew we would fall far short. We knew we could *not* be the parents to raise the first perfect child. But we also knew we had to try, both realistically and idealistically to do just that. If you set your goals low, you're pretty sure to hit them. We wanted to set them high and then do the best we could.

There was a time when I was actively interested in Summerhillian techniques of child discipline. I pretty much thought that a child left to "express itself" naturally would grow and mature in the best possible way. As I began to read Christian studies on the family and on child rearing, I learned that this concept made about as much sense as expecting a car with no driver to make it safely down a twisty, hilly, mountain road. In all of life, guidance is called for. Nothing "left to itself" will mature and grow as it will with proper and skilled guidance. An athlete needs a coach, a race horse needs a trainer and a jocky, a garden needs a gardener, a business needs a boss, and a train needs a track. Children are no different. They *need* training and guidance if they are to grow and mature properly. The Bible uses words like "deceitfully wicked above all things" to describe the human heart when left to itself.

So it is clear that training and guidance are called for. Everyone is in agreement there. Why then does the word *discipline* evoke such controversy? Why does the perspective teaching candidate sink down into his chair when the school board asks, "What is your view on discipline?" Why does he then hope he can successfully give a noncommittal answer so as not to offend any of the board members? Why are opposing opinions flaunted so freely? Why is there such heated controversy? Why does the mother of three absolute terrors, who is run ragged by them from morning to night, defensively lash back when offered some advice that might change her life? "I raised my kids the best I could and no one's gonna tell me that they coulda' done any better!"

Well, I have come to believe that an answer to all these questions lies in a basic misunderstanding of exactly what discipline is in the first place. Discipline as commonly used by the majority of people is somehow associated with angry punishment. A wrong action is punished. That is discipline. Your child breaks the vase your mother gave your wife last Christmas. You "lose your cool" and punish your child. Discipline.

Now the reason this punishment-oriented theory of discipline is such a hot subject is because our personal views of right and wrong are at stake. If I offer you a suggestion as to how you might more effectively "discipline" your child, what you hear me saying is, "I disagree with your moral value system; you don't know right from wrong."

You have no choice but to react defensively. Arguments develop, tempers flare. Nothing is ever settled because the issues involved are so basic, so deep in us. We naturally defend our position.

All of this would be avoided were we to properly understand the word discipline. The meaning of the word is much closer to guidance or training than punishment. "Punishment," however, is a key factor in effective discipline, and is a word which also needs clarification.

There are two kinds of punishment. The first is purely a response to some action. A child spills his milk. Mother slaps his hand. A thirteen-year-old leaves his father's saw outside. Father punishes him. Action followed by punishment. Responses by an angry parent are usually of this type.

The second form of punishment is redemptive. The "punishment" is not the end of the incident. It is always "looking ahead," anticipating the future. The punishment is geared toward teaching a lesson which will be valuable later on. A child disobeys and gets too near a fire. Her parents spank her, not because they are angry or even because getting near the fire was morally *wrong*. The punishment is a means of teaching her to obey and also giving her a valuable lesson which will keep her from being harmed later on. Do you see the difference? One is a quick, thoughtless response. The other is carefully planned, lovingly aimed at teaching a useful and important lesson.

This is the essence of discipline—using the second form of punishment to train a child, to provide him the guidance he needs to learn about life. This is the way God punishes. His ways are always purposeful. So must our discipline be purposeful. It cannot just be quick reactions to the mistake of our children. There is no plan in that.

But there is a lot more to *training* a child than just discipline and proper use of punishment. Training involves the whole way we relate to our children. For Judy and me it has been extremely helpful to visualize our training of Patrick and Robin in terms of "boundaries." A child must live within rigid boundaries if he is to be content and secure. As parents it is our job to establish those boundaries and then do two things.

First of all, we must give our boys all the love, affection, encouragement and praise possible within those limits. We must lose no opportunity to build confidence and security into our children through our positive approach to everything they do.

Secondly, we must strictly enforce those boundaries we set. When one of our children challenges a boundary (by disobedience or by defying our authority), then we must make absolutely certain that he pays dearly for his action. Spanking, therefore, is necessary to enforce the limits. At first this may seem arbitrary, but this is where punishment of the second type—"training"—comes in. We punish disobedience because it teaches a very valuable lesson which cannot be learned any other way.

Without this twofold approach to the limits you set for your child (building love and security within the limits, disciplining disobedience to the limits), I believe it is impossible to build love and confidence into a child. Without this approach, consistently applied, it will be very difficult for a parent to teach his child about the character of God. For God certainly operates using rigid boundaries. The Bible is the story of two kinds of people: those who accepted God's boundaries and lived according to them, and those who rejected God's laws and went their own way. The first people inherited the blessings of God; the latter, the curses. These principles of obeying (or disobeying) set standards, rules, laws, limits, and boundaries pervade all of Scripture.

This is what makes discipline as properly understood so emancipating for parents. No longer must we argue about "right and wrong" because that is no longer the basis for discipline. The basis for discipline is the setting of limits for your children. Each set of parents will arrive at their own specific limits for their children. We set individual limits. We don't need to argue; we can share and learn from each other. For various parents the limits will be different.

But there will also be certain universal qualities in the limits we as parents set. In order to be effective, boundaries must be set in advance and *must be clearly understood by the children.* If you set as a limit, "No snacking between three and six o'clock in the afternoon," then certainly you would not discipline your child for eating before he was informed of the rule. Your children must understand the boundaries. In addition, a limit must be specific and total, not vague or partial. If we say to Robin, "You must not pull Patrick's hair *hard,*" we are only inviting trouble. It must be, "Don't pull Patrick's hair *at all!*"

Whereas many of our specific limits will be different, certain limits must be universal. The most important is *defiance.* When your child willfully defies your authority, he *must* be disciplined immediately. The same is true of cold, calculating disobedience. *Respect for authority and obedience—these are absolute guidelines* set down by God himself which we must back up. These two limits are of the utmost importance. Defiance and disobedience cannot be tolerated.

But besides these, it is crucial that you *do not set so many limits that you are unable to enforce them.* It is better to enforce properly a half dozen limits than have thirty you are halfhearted about.

The problem which entraps so many Christian parents is the deception, "By being strict and uncompromising with my child, won't I be failing to love him as I should?" Many parents, therefore, try to be gentle, loving, understanding, and sympathetic to their child (all good attributes) and slowly slip into the position where the child is in control. The parent has set no

THE TWOFOLD NATURE OF BOUNDARIES AND LIMITS

within the boundaries—
love, encouragement,
affection, praise

The boundaries must be large enough to
allow the child to run, play, move,
and express himself completely without
fear.

enforce the boundaries—
when challenged, the child must pay—with
redemptive punishment

boundaries. The child has no limits on his behavior (except possibly an occasional outburst when the parents have had enough). There are no constant rules governing his actions. By giving in and allowing the child to do whatever he wants, by avoiding direct confrontations between his authority and the child's, the parent teaches the child to be in control. He is the only one that ultimately matters. He grows up not understanding authority in the least.

Such "child-controlled" parent/child relationships abound. I see them daily in our bookstore. A mother follows her youngster around, keeping him out of this and that, picking up after him, saying "no" to him time and time again. Of course the "no" carries little weight, so Junior ignores it and goes his merry way.

I grieve for these women who are on the way toward spending the whole of their child's early years frantically chasing their child about in a desperate attempt to maintain some semblance of order. The child is clearly in control and the parent is largely helpless, all because no boundaries have been set and disobedience is not dealt with. What should be some of the most joyful years of life are for such a mother a harried experience.

All this has come about because we have not been adequately taught concerning God's character and God's dealing with man. Our relationship with our children is a model of our relationship with God. And God certainly does not allow us full control. He does not give us all we desire, nor does He allow us to go our way unhindered. He knows the effect of this on us would be devastating.

The same is true with your children. We do them permanent harm by catering to their every whim and fancy. Just as God sets boundaries concerning how we are to live (boundaries which have definite and predictable consequences if ignored), we must set limits for our children and see that they are enforced.

God made us so that our only ultimate joy and satisfaction in life would come when we lived according to His laws of love. When we step outside the commandments of God, we bring harm upon ourselves. It is no different for a child. God made a child to thrive in the security and love of a family. A child is most content and happy when he knows exactly what his boundaries are. He wants the lines securely drawn. He does not want to be "free."

Why then does a child test the limits time and again? Why does he constantly disobey?

A child may test his limits for two reasons: He may be making sure they are still there. Or he may feel insecure and unsure of exactly what is expected from him and is therefore testing and pushing, trying to find out "how far he can go," to find out exactly where the boundary is. If his parents have not stood firm, a child will be insecure and will try desperately to find out "where" his parents *will* stand firm. He needs to know.

If today Mother says "no" to Junior and his disobedience is ignored, then tomorrow he will disobey again. If two "no's" followed by disobedience sometimes brings a spanking, then chances are Junior will continue to disobey until he finds *exactly* where Mom means business. If four "no's" mean *no*, and always mean *no*, then Junior will have found his secure boundary. But if Mom has given little thought to Junior lately and responds to him casually without real thought, she will probably respond according to her mood. Junior's continued disobedience, always pushing her a little further, is finally met by an angry outburst.

"What's wrong with that boy? He doesn't mind a word I say!" exclaims Mom, thinking Junior is rebellious and disobedient.

But actually poor Junior is just a little boy with a gigantic need to be loved and find security in his mother. Mom, however, is too busy and doesn't understand her son's deep need. His desperate plea goes unheeded. Every time he disobeys he is really trying to tell her, "I need your love. I need to know where my boundaries are. I'm insecure. Do you love me?"

It is a relief for a child who knows he has crossed the line to be punished. With the punishment comes the knowledge that the boundary is still there. He is secure in knowing it has held fast. When a child is consistently disciplined for disobedience to a clearly defined set of boundaries, he is submitted to an authority he knows he can trust. He knows his parents won't waver. He has tested them and they have stood firm. There is freedom and love in that obedient submission.

But even the child whose boundaries are rigid and unbending will occasionally keep trying, disobeying just to make certain the lines are still there. And if they do continue to exist, and if disobedience is clearly and painfully punished, the child will grow and mature as a happy and obedient and godly child. He is in his proper place in God's family and he knows it. He knows that his father and mother are in charge. Later he will find submission to God all the more natural because he has learned to live under the authority of his parents.

In contrast is the child who has no boundaries to govern his actions. This may occur just as easily in a Christian home as not; the principle works the same regardless of beliefs. With no boundaries, there can be no consistent discipline. As the child grows he will become increasingly disobedient in a desperate attempt to find a solid and inflexible line to trust as the limit for his actions. If he finds none, he continues to push further and further, appearing "more unruly every day." The ultimate outcome is a teenager and then adult who is submitted to no one but himself. The child who has thus controlled his parents does not respect them because he knows better than anyone they are *not* in charge. He knows he can easily twist and manipulate them, so how can he respect them? They have no backbone.

Such a child is likely to openly demonstrate this disrespect more and more as he grows older. He begins to reject his parents and everything they stand for. Since the basis for a child's response to authority comes from his relationship with his parents, a child growing up with no consistent boundaries to guide him learns disrespect. He mocks authority. Is it any wonder he cannot form a picture of God? There has been no loving, consistent authority in his background. It is foreign to him.

The Scriptures support this:

> Train up a child in the way he should go, and when he is old he will not depart from it.—Prov. 22:6 (RSV)
> A child left to himself brings shame to his mother.—Prov. 29:15 (RSV)
> Discipline your son, and he will give you rest; he will give delight to your heart.—Prov. 29:17 (RSV)
> Parents . . . bring up your children with the loving discipline the Lord approves.—Eph. 6:4 (author's par.)

Dr. Dobson cites a familiar incident between a mother and her son in which there is no consistent application of the mother's authority. Her words are empty and meaningless because she does not back them up. She has not carefully chosen to set boundaries and enforce them. Henry is fast learning to disrespect his mother.

> Eight year old Henry is sitting on the floor, playing with his games. Mom looks at her watch and says, "Henry, it's nearly nine o'clock (a thirty minute exaggeration) so gather up your junk and go take your bath." Now Henry knows, and Mom knows, that she doesn't mean for him to go take a bath. She merely means for him to start THINKING about going to take his bath. She would have fainted dead away if he had responded to her empty command. Approximately ten minutes later, Mom speaks again: "Now Henry, it is getting later and you have to go to school tomorrow, and I want those toys picked up; then go and get in that tub!" She still does not intend for Henry to obey and he knows it. Her REAL message is, "We're getting closer, Hank." Henry shuffles around and stacks a box or two to demonstrate that he heard her. Then he settles down for a few more minutes of play. Six

minutes pass, and Mom issues another command, this time
with more passion and threat in her voice, "Now listen,
young man, I told you to get a move on, and I meant
it." To Henry, this means he must get his toys picked
up and meander toward the bathroom door. If his mom
pursues him with a rapid step, however, he must carry
out the assignment post haste. However, if Mom's mind
wanders before she performs the last step of this ritual,
Henry is free to enjoy a few more seconds reprieve.

You see, Henry and his mom are involved in a one
act play; they both know the rules and the role being
enacted by the opposite player. The entire scene is pro-
grammed, computerized, and scripted. Whenever Mom
wants Henry to do something he dislikes, she progresses
through graduated steps of phony anger, beginning with
calm and ending with a red flush and a threat. Henry
doesn't have to move until she reaches the peak anger
point. How foolish this game is! Since Mom controls
him by the use of empty threats she has to stay mad all
the time. Her relationship with her children is contami-
nated, and she ends each day with a pounding, throbbing
headache. She can never count on instant obedience; it
takes her at least five minutes to work up to a believable
degree of anger.[1]

In contrast to this ineffective routine, where nothing
is accomplished except a battle of nerves, is the method
of child control where authority (the parent's words)
is enforced. The boundary clearly established through
years of practice is simple, "When I tell you to do something, you do it." Of course there are all kinds of implica-
tions to this, such as, "I will not tell you to do anything that isn't for your best"; "I will not make unrea-
sonable or embarrassing demands on you"; "I love
you and respect you as a person." The consistent parent
earns the trust and respect of his child by considerate
and loving use of his authority. But the bottom line always remains solid: "When I tell you to do something,
you do it. If you choose to disobey, you will be disciplined. I will enforce what I say. It is for your own good

I do so. I love you too much to let you disobey me and get away with it. I know that to allow that would cause you severe harm in later years as you relate to the world and to God. So believe me, if you choose to disobey, you will regret it."

A parent who consistently loves his child with this attitude does not have to get mad. The rules have been laid down well in advance. The child knows exactly what to expect. His parent follows through. He respects and loves his parents because he knows they are stronger, wiser, "tougher" than he is.

When a child does disobey willfully, the stage is set for one of the most significant learning experiences of his life. When he confronts you nose-to-nose and says, "I won't," it is not the time to sit down with him and tell him why he ought to "be a good boy and do what mommy says." Nor should he be sent to his room without dinner to pout away the evening. When a child defies you, he is really asking, "Who is in charge here, you or I?" And you must tell him. You must answer that question conclusively or he will keep asking it over and over again in more and more defiant ways. Willful disobedience must be met with physical punishment— a spanking—or it will not sufficiently answer the child's question. And when spanking is lovingly and consistently carried out at these times, very few future occasions will demand it. The child will learn the boundaries and live by them. Once the spanking is over, the child is taken in your arms and gently told why he was disciplined. That is the time to shower affection on him, so he learns that your love for him is the basis for your discipline.

A disciplined child is a contented child. No child *really* wants to be in charge. God did not give him the capacity for it. He created him to be "under" wise, loving, consistent, and strong leaders—his parents. When they back down from that responsibility, a child is frustrated. His actions may begin to look disobedient and "out of control," but inside he is crying out to be disciplined. Such conflict tears a child apart. He needs to be loved, and a good part of the love he needs is guidance and direction and boundaries to show him how to live and obey.

If only Henry's mom could see that she was teaching him rebellion and disobedience through the emptiness of her words. She is frustrated and tense, and poor Henry is gaining an unbalanced picture of life. He is now in charge. Imagine the shock several years later when he suddenly realizes that he cannot control every situation. Spanking may sound like a harsh measure for "little" acts of disobedience. But unless you begin there, how else will you avoid the major clashes later? And besides that, consider the alternatives to spanking.

On the one hand there is constant nagging and strife between parent and child. When the youngster discovers there is no threat behind the millions of words he hears, he stops listening to them. The only messages he responds to are those reaching a peak of emotion, which means there is much screaming and yelling going on ... [and the parent] often has to resort to physical punishment in the end, anyway. Thus, instead of the discipline being administered in a calm and judicious manner, the parent has become unnerved and frustrated, swinging wildly at the belligerent child. ... The situation could have ended very differently if the parental attitude had been one of confident serenity. Speaking softly, almost pleasantly, Mom says, "Henry, you know what happens when you don't mind me; now I don't see any reason in the world why I should have to make you feel pain to get your cooperation tonight, but if you insist, I'll play the game with you. When the buzzer sounds you let me know what your decision is." The child has a choice to make, and the advantages to him of obeying his mother's wishes are clear. She need not scream. She need not threaten to shorten his life. She need not become upset. She is in command. Of course, Mother will have to prove two or three times that she will apply the pain, if necessary, and occasionally throughout the coming months her child will check to see if she is still at the helm. But there is no question in my mind as to which of these two approaches involves the least pain and the least hostility between parent and child.[2]

Many Christian parents sadly think that "train up a child in the way he should go" means Sunday school, family devotions, prayer meetings, church attendance, talk about God, Bible school, and summer church camps. But unless these activities are part of a loving program of discipline—setting boundaries, clearly spelling them out to your child, and then consistently enforcing them— a child will grow up knowing a lot *about* God, while inside he does not respect his parents of the church.

If a child is taught about God as someone who must be obeyed, but through his experience at home he learns that the rules are not enforced, how can he possibly come to any understanding of obedience to God? The child will be confused. His parents tell him one thing, yet train him differently. The child naturally is in conflict and will feel the tension.

Because his view of parental authority and his respect for it forms the cornerstore for his later outlook on all authority, the underdisciplined child acquires the attitude that he need ultimately submit to *no* authority. His father, the church, his teacher, the law, society in general, those people he works with, and finally God himself—all of these he can manipulate and control. Permissive parents teach disobedience and rebellion rather than submission and obedience.

Christians instill this rebellion just as readily as anyone else. It is true that actions speak louder than words. Spiritual "words" change nothing. A child must be taught (trained) to obey.

There are two tools which, when properly and consistently applied, will work wonders to teach a young child obedience. The first is the spanking. Numerous scriptures confirm that God intends the spanking to be used in training our children. (Proverbs 22:15, 1 Samuel 2:29, Proverbs 20:30, Hebrews 12:6-7, Proverbs 23:13-14 are a very few.) This use of pain is a marvelous tool; it is one of the things a young child understands best.

> For three or four years a child accumulates bumps and bruises and scratches and burns, each one teaching him about life's boundaries. Do these experiences make him a violent person? No! The pain associated with these events teaches him to avoid making those same mistakes again. God created this mechanism [pain] as the best vehicle for a child's instruction. The loving parent can and should make use of the same processes in teaching him about certain kinds of social dangers.[3]

Another wonderful aspect about the spanking is its quickness, its conciseness. It is over in seconds! There need to be no weeks of pouting, no hurt feelings, no incindiary hostilities, no seething bitterness. Once done, it is over. Like a cut, it heals—not like a cancer which grows and festers. Bitterness and resentment are cancerous. The spanking puts an end to all those long-term, undying forms of punishment which work more ill between relationships than they solve.

> A good swift swat allow[s] tender relationships to develop immediately after [it]. The punishment is over. There is no need to stay on the outs with the child for days, or even hours. He screams and hollers and kicks and cries, then you take him into your arms. He has paid his penalty. It is over with. It is done. It is God's basic method of punishment.[4]

A spanking should be reserved for the moments of defiance, of testing the boundaries by stepping disobediently across them. It must always be done in love. It should always be consistent with previously stated limits and conditions. It should be done calmly. And a spanking should *never* be given in anger or frustration.

The second miracle-working tool at the disposal of parents for the instruction of their children is the simple word *no*. It should *never* be used lightly. It must be a word you do not carelessly fling around. It should be used only when you have the full attention of your mind on the actions of your child. Whenever you say "no" to your child, you must mean it and you must be prepared to back it up. When you say "no" and you are disobeyed, you must be prepared to spank your child. He must see that the boundary is solid—"No" means *no*!

Inconsistent use of the word no is just as damaging as arbitrary spanking. It teaches inconsistent limits. It teaches a child that his parent is wavering, indecisive, and thoughtless.

Just as bad as a thoughtless, "No, no dear, don't touch ... " as the mother moves on to something else, paying not the slightest attention to her child, is five no's followed by a spanking. In both cases a child learns that "no" might mean *no* ... but it might just mean "maybe." In any case it does not mean *no* for certain. A child is aware of this inconsistency, and it further leads to disrespect if it continues and grows.

Treat the word no as a tool. Use it carefully and thoughtfully. Do not overuse it. Use it only when you are prepared to back it up. Such use will bring great rewards in later years.

Balance is the key to all effective discipline. You must discipline consistently in love, enforcing your clearly established boundaries. Once the lines are drawn and rigidly defended, little spanking will need to be done. Too much spanking and too little spanking both have the same devastating effect on a child. They teach him that his parents are inconsistent and that the boundaries are not stable. The consistent disciplinarian finds spanking decreasingly necessary as the child matures.

* * *

As I emphasized earlier, discipline is but one aspect of the whole training process. Judy and I began to find opportunities to begin to train and teach our boys long before we had occasion to discipline them. By the time our boys were two weeks old sleep was becoming precious. I craved it. We tried every "system" we could find: both getting up with a boy, taking turns—one sleeping while the other took care of feeding both boys (this was hardly possible when Judy was nursing), or taking naps during the day. It all spelled the same thing—not enough sleep! My mom spent many nights with us, taking care of the feedings so we could get some sleep, but that obviously couldn't last forever. If the boys had been closer to "normal" (seven to eight pounds) and could have gone three or four hours between feedings, it would have been different. But two hours! and two boys to feed! I knew it couldn't last.

By about two months I was ready to get our sleeping habits back in the direction of normal. We had many friends whose nine- or ten-month-old babies still did not sleep the night through. But I knew I would never make it that far! Two things I'd heard convinced me that it didn't necessarily have to be that way. I heard that in England a newborn baby is put down for the night the first week and is not fed until morning. (I still have not found out how accurate that statement is.) And I heard that when a baby reaches eleven pounds he is physically capable of sleeping the night through without food.

Robin now weighed 10 1/2 pounds; Patrick, 9 1/2. I decided, "That's good enough for me!" It was time for their first "training." So that night I brought Robin's cradle downstairs, closed all the doors between the bedroom and living room so no one else would be disturbed, and settled onto the couch next to Robin. When he woke up hungry and crying about two hours later, I picked him up and held him. But I gave him no bottle. He cried for over an hour and eventually went back to sleep in my arms. I put him back down and went to sleep. When he awoke again, I did the same thing. And so on, until morning when I took him to Judy for some milk.

The next night I did the same thing except that I waited

a short time before picking him up. After about four nights I quit picking him up altogether and let him cry himself back to sleep. It was a difficult thing to do and I felt so "cold" sometimes. But it worked wonderfully! Within a week he was sleeping eight hours nonstop. About two weeks later I went through the same procedure with Patrick, and before long we had a somewhat normal night's sleep worked back into the schedule. In another two months both boys were going to bed at six p.m. and sleeping straight through until six or seven o'clock the following morning.

For me this was exciting! I could see the training process at work. We were starting to teach them that we were in control of their circumstances. By not giving in to their desires at every tiny peep, we began to instill the knowledge that it was not possible to have everything they wanted. I think even at this very early age such training lays the groundwork for later obedience.

I am aware that such "training" is viewed with dismay by many modern theorists of child behavior. In his book *The Emotional Needs of Children*, Dr. David Goodman writes,

> . . . [when] scheduled feeding and other strict regimens [were used] training was imposed on the child without consideration of his physiological rhythms and natural desires. And even affection was rationed in the fear that too much of it had a weakening effect on the personality. The result was a generation of neurotic, spoiled, unhappy children. . . .
>
> [Such methods teach that a child] . . . must be forced into a mold of behavior that we have set for him regardless of how unnatural it is and of how he suffers in it. And how disastrous the effect may be on his later personality! [5]

The whole basis for this trend in modern thought is that in raising children we have an "either/or" set of alternatives. This is a fallacy! Dr. Goodman writes as if "affection" and "training" are opposites. Naturally if this were true, we would have to make a choice—one or the other. But the fact is that in God's creation, love involves training. Without training and discipline, there is no love.

This is not my theory. This is God's way. The Bible says in Hebrews 12:6, "The Lord disciplines him whom he loves." Modern theory says, "Love your child and let him train himself." Dr. Goodman says, "Love comes before training," and calls rigid rules for behavior "tyranny."

Now, on the surface this is rather appealing until we stop to consider God's dealing with His people throughout all of history. God certainly has imposed "rigid rules for behavior" on us, and always has. To love our child as God loves us, we *must* train and discipline him. It is not contrary to our love; it is an intrinsic part of it. The "generation of neurotic, spoiled, unhappy children" is a result of the loss of *this aspect* of love, not the result of the loss of love. We will harm our child by trying to love without discipline *or* by trying to train without love. But when we see that love and training are *one* and are commanded of God, then we begin to see what causes a child to grow "in the fear and wisdom of the Lord."

Our choice is not between love *or* training. It is between the Lord's way (training in love) and the world's way (love OR discipline—but not both).

We have made a real effort to be sensitive to our boys' needs without catering to their crying. When there is a need, we try to meet it immediately. A baby has only one tool he can use to tell us he needs something. That is his voice. We mustn't ignore crying. It tells us very useful things. But a child has two cries—a "need-cry" and a "want-cry." Though it sometimes is very hard to tell, you must learn to distinguish between them.

A newborn baby's crying is nearly all "need-cry." Through his voice we learn of hunger, discomfort, fatigue, as well as other "difficulties." It is his only means of communicating to us. But as we meet those needs, a baby quickly learns, "Crying brings action."

So very soon the "want-cry" slowly begins to infiltrate the scene. Of course the baby is not conscious of all this taking place. He just knows, "When I cry, somebody comes and picks me up, and I like to be held." So it is quite natural for him to cry when you put him down. He is not belligerent or disobedient or rebellious; he just likes you to hold him.

Now I can understand that. In fact, I like very much to hold my boys. But I know two additional things. One, I know that I cannot hold them all day long. Two, I know they must learn that the universe does not revolve around our wants. So I realize my need to train my boys even if it means the temporary hurt of having to let them cry when they would rather be held and I would like to hold them.

I hope it doesn't sound as if I never held my boys when they were very young. Whenever I had a spare minute, I would grab one of them to carry around with me. I walked them to sleep, carried them, played with them, and lay on the floor, letting them crawl all over me. My point is simply this—they needed to learn lessons they could learn no other way than through my occasional ignoring of their purely "want-cries." In not catering to their every want, I believe we were teaching the first elemental truths concerning the attributes of God. And in addition I believe we were preparing them for the times in the future when we would place restrictions on their behavior. I did not want the first "no" to be the first time in their life they ever encountered a barrier to their desires. So I looked on these early lessons as healthy preparation for more direct training in the future.

When the boys reached a more active and mobile age (six to nine months), Judy and I found ourselves often having to stop to evaluate the reason behind a cry. If it was a "need-cry," then we had to take appropriate action—put him down for a nap even though it wasn't time, because he was sleepy; get lunch ready; check to see if the diaper needed changing, loosen Robin's grip on Patrick's hair. But if no apparent need was present, then we had to plan our action on the basis of a "want-cry."

We have taken Dobson's advice and stood outside their room waiting for the moment of silence to rush in and pick them up, thereby rewarding the quiet rather than the crying. We have experimented by picking up a crying boy. If he stops and then starts up again when we begin to put him back down, then we have a fairly clear idea that he just wants to be held. We try not to come running every time we hear a cry. (Unless it is an obvious emergency—like the time I heard a loud *bump* and then a scream. Patrick had been put to sleep in the middle of a large bed. He could hardly crawl two feet at the time. But somehow he managed to inch over to the edge after waking up and just toppled right over the edge. When I ran in I found a frightened Patrick looking around for someone to explain this latest lesson to him—gravity!) We don't want to give them the idea, "When I cry the world stops and everyone comes running to take care of me." Even most "need-cries" don't have to receive instant and frantic attention. It is good to react to crying in a calm manner. That makes it all the easier later to extinguish fussy crying and reward good behavior.

It is not easy to determine what is behind a cry many times. There are no simple solutions. Each set of parents must get to know their own children individually. At four months Patrick entered a time of extreme fussiness. We thought he was beginning to get ornery. It later turned out he had a severe double hernia and was in excruciating pain. Teething also causes much fussiness and irritability. It is a painful time when the body is out of balance. Babies need a lot of holding and comforting and rocking and walking at that time. Sleepiness also causes fussiness. It's no good trying to "train" and "discipline" a baby who is just plain tired.

There are countless other causes of genuine "need-cries." Each child has its own signs. It is easy to get out of balance in either direction—too much attention, too little attention. You must simply be on your toes. Raising children cannot be done casually. For a small child every moment of his life is a learning experience. We are always teaching something. If we act without thinking, he learns nonetheless—possibly a new way to manipulate us. And so often this occurs without our slightest awareness.

There is often overlap between needs and wants. Occasionally one of the boys would get frightened and cry. When picked up he would stop. But that was no indication he was just crying to get his own way. He was afraid and needed the comfort of being held closely. Babies need the security of arms wrapped tightly around them. I am in no way advocating that we lessen the affection we shower upon our children. I am simply saying that affection *alone* will not teach a child to grow up to be a responsible person who loves and fears the Lord. Our affection must be thoughtful and must contain training and teaching.

I want to be sensitive to my children. I want to understand what they are actually experiencing in their own little world. I remember wishing I could become small enough to get into their crib with them, just to see and understand what the world looked like to them. As we learn to see through their eyes we will become more effective in our teaching and discipline.

There was a time of about a week when Patrick suddenly couldn't sleep for more than four hours. At first, thinking he just wanted to be picked up, we tried to ignore him. After several nights, however, it became apparent it was a need-cry. It was different. We knew something was wrong but we had no idea what. We tried an extra bottle, but that didn't help either. We had no idea.

It was during a cold spell so we finally thought, "Maybe he could be cold." We turned up the thermostat and immediately the problem was solved. You must get to know your child and experiment gently and sensitively with him.

There are multitudes of opportunities where good teaching tools exist. There have been times since the boys have been sleeping through the night when one of them would wake up for some unexplained reason. The natural thing to do is get up and rock him or give him a bottle. But we have carefully tried not to cater or give in to it. After making sure everything was in order (the diaper changed, the fright subsided), we simply turned him back over on his stomach and left him to go back to sleep. We have never regularly gotten them out of bed. We knew to do so could unlearn the habit of sleeping regularly through the night.

Eating habits provide another area where great learning can be accomplished. I'm not up on the pro's and con's of "demand" feeding versus "schedule" feeding. But I do know with twins there is nothing but schedule feeding. Not only from a time standpoint, but I think schedule feeding teaches young children something from the moment they are born. It teaches them that there is something greater than they to be reckoned with— *the schedule!* The world doesn't jump at their every call. It is patterned after a prescribed order which can be depended on. They must conform to the rules.

But in this, as in everything with children, there can be no dogmatic and final answers. Flexibility is the by-word with young children (especially with *twins!*). These principles must be applied to different individuals who are going to respond differently. Sensitivity to their personal differences and needs will largely determine the specifics of how each set of parents carries them out.

Above all, what we try to do with Patrick and Robin is to stay in charge ourselves. It is they who must conform to our lives, not us to theirs. We want to carefully and prayerfully select the boundaries we place around them. We attempt to place a minimum number of restrictions on them, and then prepare ourselves to enforce the rules strictly. We realize that we will face changes and will have to adapt as new things come up. But the changes and flexibility necessary are in the specifics. The framework of boundaries and their importance in training remain firm.

When the boys reached nine months, two things happened which told me more direct forms of discipline were close at hand. First of all, they began to crawl with some proficiency; and secondly, I could see in their eyes that first glimmer of "knowing." I don't know exactly how to describe what I mean by that. I had known all along it would have been futile ever to spank or say "no" to Robin or Patrick unless they had some capability for grasping what was going on. That would be senseless and cruel. But once they could understand, however slight, something of what was going on, then genuine teaching could occur. I had a feeling I would be able to "see" this germ of comprehension in their faces even though I didn't exactly know what I was looking for.

With the advent of their housewide mobility, having some boundaries now became necessary. We had two choices—either we could move out of their reach everything we didn't want them to touch, or we could "teach" them what they couldn't get into. Having seen that first glimmer of insight in their eyes, we both felt they were now capable of learning to restrict themselves. So we decided to begin the discipline and training process with a compromise. We would carefully choose certain things to leave within their grasp which we wouldn't allow them to touch. Then we would remove the other problem things. We chose to make an issue of a few selected things. We limited the boundaries we wanted them to have to cope with.

The first issue came over a plugged-in extension cord, obviously a dangerous item for a child to chew on. We left one very tempting cord right where it belonged and removed all the others. The next day, Robin approached the cord. Judy said slowly, making sure he was alert and fixed on her voice, "Robin . . . no!" and then picked him up and moved him away. Having not heard the word "no" before, Robin first had to learn that "no" meant not touching. So lesson one was just to move him away.

The next day he again headed for the cord.

"Robin . . . no!" Robin hesitated, looked up at Judy with obvious debate going on in his little brain. He had learned already. Then he grabbed the cord and started to chew on it. Judy slapped his hand (not hard) and moved him away. He cried, but from frustration and emotional "hurt," not physical pain.

Two days later, Robin approached the cord, hesitated, looked up at Judy, and then moved on to something else.

Now of course I don't hastily conclude from this that Robin suddenly knew what "no" meant and will always obey. Hardly! Six months later we still found ourselves having to go through the same process right from the beginning. A young child is slow to learn regular obedience. But this inability always to do what we say isn't necessarily disobedience either.

In a very young child the two are not always distinctively opposite. They are constantly exploring, testing, questioning, seeking answers.

This doesn't lessen our need or our responsibility to be aware of their persistent learning. We must be constantly, yet gently, teaching them as they grow. Every little move a nine-month-old baby makes cannot always be seen as either obedience or disobedience. Sometimes he will seem to obey, other times not. But often it is neither; it is experimentation. He is learning about the world, you, language, boundaries, and objects. However, the older a child becomes, the sharper the distinction becomes between obedience and defiance. Through these first initial incidents I saw that much learning was already taking place in Patrick and Robin. I could see more clearly all the time my need to be consistent, thoughtful, and attentive—and always in love.

About three days later, Patrick encountered the cord. Much the same thing happened. He had previously had the "no" and been removed from the temptation, so now he was ready for his first encounter with physical discipline. Judy said "no," Patrick went ahead for the cord, and received a mild slap on his hand.

Just after that incident Judy called me at the bookstore.

"It's so exciting," she bubbled. *"It works!"*

And that's my only defense of this method and these thoughts when all has been said and written—it works! I fear that many of the books written today and many of the theories developed originate in quiet offices somewhere far removed from children and further removed from the teachings of the Bible. For one look at any public elementary school today where permissiveness reigns will tell you that rebellious and uncontrolled children are a direct result of an "unworkable" theory. The final proof must be, "Does it work?"

One morning during the same week of the cord incidents, after being fed, Patrick started to fuss and cry. We checked all the usual items to make sure he was okay, but the crying continued. It was clearly not a need-cry. When it got worse and worse, and when I saw that he was just being cranky and stubborn, I put him back down in his bed. That really did it! He hollered and complained like never before.

I knew discipline was going on. No spanking, no disobedience, yet it was training nevertheless. I let him cry. It was hard for me to do, especially since it went on for at least twenty minutes. Eventually it softened and the moment it stopped I rushed in to get him. For the next hour he sat contentedly in my lap playing and quietly talking to himself. He was happy and at peace. He had discovered that someone stronger was in charge and he was secure in that.

Now it could be said that I am going to stiffle his growth and personality with such actions. It could be said that my children will fear me and cower before me. It could be said that their natural creativity and imagination will not have a chance to grow because of the rigid boundaries I impose on them.

It is possible to *say anything*, but what we say must be proved in practice. "Does it work?" And when I walk into the boys' room in the morning, or come home at night, or come upon them unexpectedly at some other time, the look on their faces tells me, "Something *right* is happening!" When they see me they come alive with excitement. They love me! They respond the same to Judy. There is no fear of their growth being crushed under this system. It is flowering and maturing because this is God's way. Being a father is exciting to me especially for this reason—I can see the pinciples *working*. No longer are they book, office, seminar, theoretical dogmas. They are the fabric of the life we live daily with our boys.

The message of the Psalms is repeatedly, "The ways of the Lord are perfect." This is true in every aspect of life, especially in the Lord's commands regarding the raising of our children. His clear injunction is, "Train up a child in the way he should go, and when he is old he will not depart from it." It is our responsibility to point him "the way he should go." To fail to do this directly disobeys the very word of God.

12

Life with Twins

The recurring comment we get from mothers of young children is, "I can't *imagine* what it must be like to raise twins!" And nearly everyone asks, "What is it like?"

The answer is simple. "It is a lot of work!"

There are unique circumstances involved with twins in just about every imaginable detail of life. To think that merely doubling the effort is all that is required is a tremendous understatement. Twins present a host of unusual circumstances which are not found in single children. This is true in every area—feeding, clothing, bathing, discipline, learning, sleeping. "During the first year they require from 1 1/2 to 3 times the work and strain involved in raising a single born infant." [1]

Prior to the birth of our boys we read up on everything we could find to help us practically prepare for what faced us. One of the most helpful books we discovered in the library (now out of print) was *Twice the Trouble, Twice the Fun* by Betsy Gehman. Her one suggestion which I can profess to as the most helpful piece of equipment possible for handling twins is an octopus. There just aren't enough hands to do what needs to be done!

The first three months were hectic! It is just a matter of learning to "cope" to get through those days.

As Judy has said many times, "You do what you

have to do," and that is about it. You just do.

Since that time, however, life became somewhat "routine" again. Once the boys were sleeping twelve to thirteen hours a night, we again had our evenings and nights to relax, recover, sleep, and prepare for another day. Believe me, that was tremendous! "R and R!"

During the first six to nine months we discovered certain things we had to do to help retain a balanced life and to keep the care of the boys from becoming a rut. It was important for Judy to get out of the house once in a while. For a short time we had a babysitter come regularly twice a week for two or three hours. This freed Judy to go shopping or visiting or to come to the store. One day Judy was so itchy just to "get out of the house" she practically begged me to let her go pick up some saw blades I was having sharpened. These "off" times, though few, rejuvenated her spirit and helped her ready herself for the daily tasks again.

During those months Judy was severely limited. She couldn't go anywhere with the twins without another adult along. But as the boys gradually could do and understand more, it became easier for her to do things with them. We have a double stroller, and I attached two seats on the back of an old three-wheeler bike. So when the weather was nice Judy began to take the boys for afternoon walks or bike rides. They enjoyed it so much (singing to themselves, talking and waving to everyone they passed, getting so excited at the sight of a cat or dog they would try to climb right out of their seat) that it soon became a daily adventure.

Occasionally, for a change of pace, Judy would ride or walk down to the store with the boys in the afternoon. Then she and I'd switch places for the remainder of the day. She would close up the store and I would take the boys home and give them their dinner. It provided a break from the routine for us both.

It has also been helpful for Judy to have an extra project going (sewing a new dress, redoing a room, embroidering a Christmas present). Of course these are extra and do not take her away from the children. But they provide her a creative way to accomplish something lasting—beyond the daily grind of bottles, diapers, dishes, dirty clothes, housecleaning. In the endless succession of daily tasks, it is uplifting to make something you know will *get done*, and which you won't have to face the next morning all over again. It is encouraging to see and appreciate and use something you've made. The accomplishment is lasting.

I have seen that being a mother has drained Judy emotionally. She loves being a mother. I never cease to be amazed at how excited she always is about playing and talking with the boys. But I can see the drain too. Therefore I know it is important for us to stress some of the "finer things." Her spirit needs it. Getting dressed up, going somewhere to visit, going out, going to church—these are all activities that give Judy a new burst of enthusiasm. I need to be sensitive to that aspect of her life. I need to provide her opportunities to "be a woman" as well as a mother.

Above all we continually see our need to be a family. At the center is our marriage relationship. Our children are aware of the flow between us. If there is the slightest tension, they feel it immediately. Our relationship to one another is the basis for Patrick's and Robin's view of the world. We must give and give and give and never stop giving to one another.

As a couple, the boys are our priority. All else (time, money, career, church, the store) has to fall in line behind them. It may sound like an easy decision, but I find I must continually reaffirm it. The hardest part of it is time. It means sitting on the floor with them, talking to them, holding them, reading to them. And both Judy and I are so active, just slowing down to do these simple things takes an effort.

One special time we have together is in the morning. When the boys were very young we got into the habit of getting them up and feeding their morning bottle to them in our bed. Then when finished we would play with them there until they became restless. When they were older the play occupied our entire bedroom. We would crawl around investigating every little new and unusual corner with them. It has become a "family time" to start the day.

As the months lengthened it was fascinating to see the boys' understanding and comprehension increasing. By twelve and fourteen months it was clear they definitely knew the meaning of many words and were aware of many of the boundaries we had set. Their learning process was often comical.

The garbage can in the kitchen, for instance, was a "no" from the start, and they certainly knew it very soon. But for months it seemed they had to daily test it. No matter how many times their probing and inquisitive hands were slapped following a "no," they would come back for more.

But the funny thing was to see how clever they became. Not mischievous yet, but humorously alert and clever. Robin discovered he could back up to the garbage can and touch it with his back and thereby conceal his overt interest in it. Then he ventured to lean his head back to touch it. And from there it was a simple matter to quietly sneak his hand back over his shoulder onto it, all the while looking distractedly in the other direction as if to say, "I really am not the least bit aware of this garbage can and could care less." Such a subtle procedure to investigate the limit!

Judy and I just have to laugh to watch their active little minds at work. It is fun. It must be taken seriously, but in perspective. Much of the testing is humorous at this point, not defiance. They are just learning and discovering with every ounce of energy they have. It is possible to get so wrapped up in one aspect of raising a child that you fail to see the good natured capriciousness surrounding their every exploratory little move. You must keep sight of the balance between "what a cute little fellow he is" and what incredible and significant things he is learning. We thoroughly enjoy both aspects.

Walking that middle ground has been more interesting the older Patrick and Robin have become. The hearth is another "no" place. But how they love to skirt the edges of it, hoping, it seems, they will "accidentally" fall right on it. And the hand that just "happens" to land on some forbidden object (like Judy's music stand) while the obviously uninterested boy gazes in the opposite direction. Yes, learning is going on constantly—by both parents and children! You've got to be on your toes.

And learning is also going on in your play with them. Patrick loved to bait Judy or me into chasing him. Sitting on his haunches looking out of the corner of his eye, just waiting. Then at your first move off he would go (he could crawl faster than any child I've ever seen) down the hall. But every second or two his head would swing around just enough for him to glance back to make sure you were still there. And when you were not only there but gaining, out would gush a rolling giggle as he tore off even faster.

But our boys are different. Robin never liked to be chased at all. He had his own little games. We could see so many differences we often wondered, "Are they really identical?" (No tests were ever done; it was merely assumed.) But then when I am holding Robin but talking to Patrick and Judy says, "Mike, that's Robin," then we think they must be. It is always good for a laugh when one of us catches the other in a a mistaken identity! It's not usually how much they look alike. It's just that occasionally Robin gets a particularly Patrick look on his face or Patrick does some peculiarly Robin thing. Then it does become confusing.

I think one of the things that makes twins so fun is the two of them scurrying about all the time—not so much what they do. But they're like two little kittens playing—funny just by nature. I think all young children are inherently funny and cute. New parents from the beginning of time have laughed over the antics of their children. When the boys first learned to climb onto a chair, we came into a room to find Patrick sitting like an adult quietly and still in the middle of a rocker ten times his size. And after Robin discovered his nose, we would find him sitting with a finger or two lodged in his nostrils. Exploring a new food (like a grape) is always fun to watch. The probing finger lightly touches it, withdraws, then extends itself again, uncertain, prodding. And we had to laugh, but with a degree of fright, to walk into the dining room only to find Patrick perched atop the table, wondering how he got there. And how he was going to get down. If a place is unattainable to them, they just try all the harder to get there. And they often do. Fear seems to be completely absent. They must explore the unknown, the unreachable, no matter what or where it is.

At about the time the boys learned to walk (fifteen months), it seemed as if they were suddenly able to understand much of what we said. If the words "breakfast," "bath," or "dinner" accidentally popped out, off they would go lickity split to the bathroom or kitchen. It's amazing what they're able to pick up, and how soon.

They are sometimes cranky and difficulty. It is not always *fun*. I cannot honestly say I *always* feel like giving my boys my time and energy. I get tired. But children need their parents and so I know I must *always* be willing immediately to drop anything if at all possible to spend time with my boys. It is so easy to neglect a child because his world is so small and unimportant to us. But a hurt finger or a bruise or a new discovery is important to your child—earth shattering! I pray I never lose sight of that. I have even tried getting down on the floor and imagining I see the piece of string Patrick had in his mouth as he sees it. I imagined I was asking him about it and he was telling me about his discovery. "This string tastes good, Dad!" He was sucking on it with such a passion, it must have. I want to be in the habit of seeing through Patrick's and Robin's eyes. I pray my being bigger doesn't cloud my vision. To understand them I must be capable of living on their level.

13

Through a Child's Eyes

In the Training Manual for our book shop I tell my employees that the success of our business depends upon our being able to "see through the customer's eyes." We must be so sensitive to his needs that we fully appreciate all he feels as he enters our store. Only then can we be in a position to truly minister to him.

The same principle applies in relating to our children. If I am to make one dogmatic statement, which I doubt I shall ever change, it is this: Confidence, security, and love are built into a child by his parents' seeing through his eyes. This does not negate our need to train our children, even train them in ways often unpleasant to them. Indeed, my ability to see through my child's eyes must be at the root of my training. There will often be times when my maturity combined with my being able to see through his eyes will make me more aware of his deepest needs than he is.

So if I find it necessary to spank my child, it is not that I don't understand things from his viewpoint and am treating him cruelly. On the contrary! It is because I am aware of what is in his heart when he disobeys me and I see (better than he does) his long-range, deep need to have that rebellion eliminated. It is only the parent that truly has trained himself to see through his child's eyes who can effectively train and guide the child according to the child's deepest needs.

And similarly it is only by seeing through a child's eyes that we can feed and nurture the curiosity and imagination and energy God put in him, and cause those traits to grow into confidence, security and creativity. Our responses to our child will largely crush or build up the boundless and energetic resources found in him. If we stimulate, encourage, listen to, and talk with our children *on their level*, seeing their world in the exciting and fresh ways they see it, we will enhance and nourish their creative growth. But if we do not take the time to "be" with them in *their* world—if we remain as an "adult," not penetrating their *real lives*—then we will suppress and ultimately kill their childish exuberance and spontaneity. Unencouraged and stifled children grow up unproductive and lethargic, with feelings of inferiority and little self-confidence. We, the parents, hold the power to either make or break our child's self-esteem by the way we are to him in the little moments of every day.

Perhaps an example will clarify what I mean. I saw this incident recently in our store. A father was deeply engrossed in a book. His daughter found her way to the trinket shelf, scanned it quickly, picked up a balloon and walked over to her father.

"Daddy, can I have a balloon?"

Silence.

"Daddy . . . "

"Yes, dear, what is it?" he said without looking up.

"Can I have a balloon?"

After a pause . . . "A what?"

"A balloon."

"Oh . . . " Another pause. "I don't know," he sighed, finally tearing his eyes from the page in front of him.

"Did you ask your mother?"

So it goes. The father isn't paying any attention to his daughter and could care less about her balloon. He is more interested in the discussion of systematic theology before him than his daughter's balloon. His eyes are for himself, not for her.

So many parents have not the slightest inkling of what goes on in their son's or daughter's head from day to day. An incident such as this usually ends at the cash register with the man buying both his book and his daughter's balloon. To get her off his back he finally yields.

"And why not?" he would ask. "If she wants it I'll get it for her."

But what has this little girl learned from all this? She has seen first of all that Daddy isn't too interested in what she is interested in and would rather read books. Secondly, she has learned that she can usually get what she wants if she bugs Mommy and Daddy long enough. Not only is she learning to withdraw into herself from lack of parental interest and stimulation, she is learning how to be in control.

And I am afraid that often I am no better. Getting outside myself is no easy matter. I find my constant prayer must be, "Lord, open my eyes!"

We teach our children all day long, usually without realizing it. We quickly convey to them our lack of interest in their affairs. But if we have any hope of overcoming the "epidemic of inferiority" in our own children, it can come only through being genuinely interested in their little lives—seeing through their eyes; being able to live with them on their level. This means far more than just allotting some time each day to spend with them. It means really "getting into them," where they tick.

There are all kinds of areas where we have the opportunity to instill self-esteem and confidence into our children. But it takes constant awareness and a constant denial of the world's values to recognize them. Our vocal responses are a key example. It is so easy to criticize without thinking.

"Is that all the better you can do? I know you can do better!"

That's a common parental evaluation.

We somehow think that we are going to uncover hidden talents by saying his immediate work is below par.

"Spur him on!" we say.

But every such criticism is a blow to the self-image of a child. When multiplied by the number of times he receives such comments throughout his lifetime, we produce a lazy, boring, unproductive man with inferiority feelings stretching back to the cradle.

But with every little compliment we build an inner confidence and strength that enables a man to accomplish great things because he has a secure and positive self-image.

* * *

Applying these principles with twins has been complicated for us.

> At the very start of their lives twins do come up against a unique circumstance: Each enters a world in which a competing baby of exactly the same age is always present, always making equal demands, and always as a rule being given equal treatment. Each twin sees and feels that he is not the only pebble on the beach.[1]

Of course there is the tremendous benefit from this that twins know almost instinctively that they cannot always be the center of attention. There are two of them to go around rather than just one. They often have to wait their turn long before a single child would have to.

But the most severe problem involving twins, which is an extremely important obstacle for their parents to overcome, is individuality, especially when dealing with self-esteem and confidence. If twins are forever lumped into the same mold, opportunities for them to create and express themselves as individuals will be less frequent. And such experiences are necessary to self-confidence.

This is vital, not only with twins, but also with all children. A child must develop as an individual person. We've got to care, take time, experience things with him as a *person*, as the unique individual God made him.

He must sense his uniqueness, his specialness to blossom as he should. This is where hobbies, sports, music, reading, crafts, interests of all kinds are so vital in children's lives. Success experience *as an individual* is important to every child. We must see that they get it. From our daily living with them to the major activities they engage in, *there must be success!* Success builds confidence.

Small doses of failure teach us to cope with life. There must be a healthy balance of each. But the foundation must be built on confidence. We give our children confidence by making their lives a success. One child may be an athlete, one a musician, one may tie fishing flies. But succeed they must! And that success is measured by our response. They must know that to us, *they're the best in the world!*

We try to encourage and stimulate Patrick and Robin in positive ways. When they try, reach, grasp we make sure they succeed. Parents make the attempt successful by their response more than by the effort of the child. Even a minor and incomplete action, if treated properly by a parent, becomes a gigantic accomplishment which builds confidence and further motivates a child.

When Patrick was learning to crawl we would put him on the floor a foot or two away from us and then reach out encouraging him to come. He would struggle and twist and moan and reach in an unreserved and whole-hearted effort. After only a few inches sometimes he would start to get frustrated. But no matter how little the "visible" progress we always made sure that in the end he "made it" by sweeping him up in a big hug of praise.

Praise motivates while criticism tears down. I see my need to be in the habit of praising and complimenting for the effort rather than the results. I don't want to be guilty of meeting Robin at the door and seeing his first-grade picture of a cow in a field clutched proudly in his hand, only to say, "Oh, you can do better than that." I hope when that moment comes (through years of practice) I will naturally exclaim, "Robin! Did YOU

draw *that*? *Wow*! Tell me about it." (Not, "What is it?")
We must communicate worth to our children on the basis
of who they are as God's child—worthwhile, capable, significant, and loved.

There are so many ways we can tear down a child's
self-esteem. Teasing, sarcasm, comparing, always expecting "better." We can aim high, yes. But when an
effort is made, we must be excited about the result.
Compliments and praise cannot be made lightly, however;
they must be genuine. Success must be related to the
effort, not to less significant externals. Praise and encouragement are absolutely vital to a healthy confidence
and self-image in a child. So we mustn't lose any opportunity to get down on our knees with our child and get
interested in his world. Everything looks so different from
where he is standing. And as we do it we cannot be dis-
tracted or absorbed. Our interest must be real.

Time is so important to a child. There is *no* substitute.
We must spend time with our children, lots of it. Parents
have enormous power to damage or build the confidence
and self-esteem of their children. And the most vital factor
in cultivating our capacity to see through their eyes is
spending interested, excited time with them, doing with
them what they like to do. There is nothing so exciting
to a child as to have his father go to the fort with him,
play ball with him, or see the new dress she made for
her doll. A child wants more than anything to incorporate
you into his life.

Giving a child responsibility is an important tool in
the building of self-esteem and confidence. A baby comes
into the world with no responsibilities and leaves home
some twenty years later expected to carry the full responsibility for all areas of his life. In the years between
it is the job of the parents to prepare him for the task.
This must begin in infancy with the transferring of tiny
responsibilities from parent to child. Throughout childhood the responsibilities gradually increase.

We must be especially careful and attentive in our

training and discipline whenever we are also giving new responsibilities to our children. Increasing responsibility also allows for the possibility of irresponsible behavior. And we must keep ever before us the tremendous difference between disobedience and childish irresponsibility. Exploration and experimentation are vital in the child's learning process and play a part in his understanding what responsibility means. If we discipline our child for pure childishness in the same way we discipline disobedience, we will ultimately smother his curious instinct. And this is one of the greatest teachers he has.

So, though in the emotion of the moment it may often be difficult to distinguish, it would be harmful to spank a child for irresponsibility. When a glass of milk is accidentally spilled, when a vase is accidentally knocked on the floor, you should take the opportunity to teach your child to be more responsible. But you should not discipline him in the same way you would had he defiantly challenged you.

Dobson contrasts defiance with childish irresponsibility as follows:

> ... defiant behavior ... is headstrong and willful. It is premeditated and calculating ... It is intentional, and deserves immediate disciplinary action.[2]

Again the key is being able to see as our child sees. If he is rebelling, we must deal with his disobedience. But if he is just honestly learning about his world, we cannot punish him because he happens to cross some line he knew nothing about. His intention tells the story. And to know that we must be extremely sensitive to his heart and his viewpoint. Unjust discipline and thoughtless punishment will undermine our relationship with our child quicker than anything.

Therefore the setting of limits is crucial. The wise parent will establish his limits with care, choosing few enough so that his child has freedom to express all his natural curious desires (reach, touch, bite, grab, taste, lick, shake) without constant oversight. This curiosity is not hostile or aggressive. It is the process for learning which God put into little children.

I have seen parents slap their two year old throughout the day for simply investigating his world. This squelching of normal curiosity is not fair to the youngster. It seems foolish to leave an expensive trinket where it will tempt him, and then lash him for taking the bait. If little fat-fingers insists on handling the china cups on the lower shelf, then it is much wiser to distract him with something else than to pound him for his persistence. ... Spankings should be reserved for his moments of greatest antagonism ... the toddler years are critical to the child's future attitude toward authority. He should be patiently taught to obey without being expected to behave like an adult ...

Too often our parental instruction consists of a million "don'ts" which are jammed down the child's throat. We should spend more time rewarding him for the behavior we do admire, even if our "reward" is nothing more than a sincere compliment. Remembering the child's need for self-esteem and acceptance, the wise parent can satisfy those important longings while using them to teach valued concepts and behavior.[3]

Seeing through a child's eyes means respecting him and his interests at every age and stage. Recognizing his characteristics, realizing he *needs* to crawl, explore, pry, play. Obviously a small child is disruptive to an adult schedule if it hasn't been geared to include him. But we must ask ourselves every day, "What is my priority today? My schedule, my work, my rest? or my son?" Thoughtless parents think of their own needs while overlooking the needs of their children which are *just as important to the child* as the parents' are to them.

Time is so important to our children. The most important lessons of a child's life are learned during the small, unimportant times we are with them. They know how we look at those times. If they are an "interruption" to us, then to a child we don't really care. Our ability to live with them, enjoy what they enjoy, see as they see is the key to a child's emotional development.

When I look back on my childhood, I am reminded first of all of times with my parents. Times like my dad throwing passes to me in the backyard. ("If your fingers touch it, you should have it.") How I would love it when he would say, "Good catch!" Times before school when he would call out my spelling words to me. The time when my mom worked with me learning to ride a bike so we could surprise Dad with my progress when he came home from the shop. The time when my dad and Cathy came to watch me run in a track meet, and when I got home at one in the morning I found a note on my bed from my mom, saying, "Congrats—3rd'er!"

My parents were interested, they spent time with Cathy and Janet and me. Yet in talking with them now I find that in the early years of my dad's business he often had to work until midnight. I don't remember that, nor do I know where he found the time to read to me. But he took the time and I know it had its effect on my later development. That's the kind of father I want to be.

Many necessary attributes toward self-esteem are summed up by George MacDonald in his novel *The Vicar's Daughter*. I'd like to share his wisdom with you.

First for a few negative principles.

1. Never give in to disobedience; and never threaten what you are not prepared to carry out.
2. Never lose your temper. I do not say never be angry. Anger is sometimes indispensable, especially where there has been anything mean, dishonest, or cruel. But anger is very different from loss of temper.
3. Of all things, never sneer at them; and be careful, even, how you rally them.
4. Do not try to work on their feelings. Feelings are far too delicate things to be used for tools. It is like taking the mainspring out of your watch, and notching it for a saw. It may be a wonderful saw, but how fares your

watch? Especially avoid doing so in connection with religious things, for so you will assuredly deaden them to all that is finest. Let your feelings, not your efforts or their's, affect them with a sympathy the more powerful that it is not forced upon them; and, in order to do this avoid being too English in the hiding of your feelings. A man's own family has a right to share in his good feelings.

5. Never show that you doubt, except you are able to convict. To doubt an honest child is to do what you can to make a liar of him; and to believe a liar, if he is not altogether shameless, is to shame him.

6. Instill no religious doctrine apart from its duty. If it have no duty as its necessary embodiment, the doctrine may well be regarded as doubtful.

7. Do not be hard on mere quarrelling, which, like a storm in nature, is often helpful in clearing the moral atmosphere. Stop it by a judgment between the parties. But be severe as to the kind of quarrelling, and the temper shown in it. Especially give no quarter to any unfairness arising from greed or spite. Use your strongest language with regard to that.

Now for a few positive rules.

1. Always let them come to you, and always hear what they have to say. If they bring a complaint, always examine it, and dispense pure justice, and nothing but justice.

2. Cultivate a love of giving fair-play. Every one, of course, likes to receive fair-play; but no one ought to be left to imagine, therefore, that he loves fair-play.

3. Teach from the very first, from the infancy capable of sucking a sugar plum, to share with neighbors. Never refuse the offering a child brings you, except you have a good reason—and give it. And never pretend to partake: that involves hideous possibilities in its effect on the child.

The necessity of giving a reason for refusing a kindness has no relation to what is supposed by some to be the necessity of giving a reason with every command. There is no such necessity. Of course there ought to be a reason in every command. It may be desirable, sometimes, to explain it. But not always.

4. Allow a great deal of noise,—as much as is fairly endurable; but the moment they seem to be getting beyond their own control, stop the noise at once. Also put a stop at once to all fretting and grumbling.

5. Favor the development of each in the direction of his own bent. Help him to develop himself, but do not push development. To do so is most dangerous.

6. Mind the moral nature, and it will take care of the intellectual. In other words, the best thing for the intellect is the cultivation of the conscience, not in casuistry, but in conduct. It may take longer to arrive; but the end will be the highest possible health, vigor, and ration of progress.

7. Discourage emulation, and insist on duty,—not often, but strongly.

14

The Last Word

As I consider how to most effectively conclude what I have to say to you, I keep asking myself, "What will give it that final zing? What can I say that will so motivate these readers that they'll go out and apply these principles in their own families?"

But then I must retreat a step and ask, "But is that really the best way to wrap it up?" If some extra "zing" were the way to motivate readers, then why would Larry Christenson have begun *The Christian Family* with an explanation of his deliberately dull title? It must have been because he had a message which he wanted to say with no frills attached. And that is how I want to leave you, with a message firmly embedded in your understanding. With no frills.

What is a "Christian family in action"? Is it a family who has it all worked out? Is it a family whose barriers and obstacles and trials are things of the past? Hardly! It is simply a family (a Christian one) that is actively trying to live by the principles of the Bible in their daily lives. Our family is no different from your family. The only difference is that I have written a book about ours. In that sense we are sort of a "test case" to see how this thing works. We have opened up our windows to let you see into our lives for a while. But otherwise there is no distinction.

I encourage you to remember that. You have read this book. You have read about us. You have seen God at work in our family—not in our sufficiency nor in our wisdom, but in spite of our failings and limited faith. God can work in your family in the same way. No matter what the situation may be, and no matter how small you may think your faith is, God is able to do great things in your specific circumstances. But it won't happen automatically. You must be diligent in applying the principles.

And that is no simple matter! To diligently follow through to the end of anything takes work. And let's face it. Life is not basically an easy proposition. God has never promised that we'd float through it. Life is largely a struggle. But God has laid down some rather clear guidelines to help us in all areas of life. In this case we're talking about the family. But in every aspect of life there are principles which God has established. Whether you're a Christian or not, if the principles are applied the results will be predictable.

I'm in business and I understand that certain principles lead to certain results. It is true for the non-Christian enterprise as well as the Christian one. If a Christian, through sloppy management and poor planning, fails in a business venture, it is pointless for him to ponder, "What happened? I thought the Lord was leading me into this." He can't lazily place the responsibility for his failure in the Lord's hands when he simply didn't adhere to good sound business principles.

In the same way, if you are having some family difficulties, it is no good praying day after day for God to take them away if you are unwilling to make a daily and concerted effort (yes, work!) to live by and do what the Bible specifies. You must diligently follow the principles.

This has been the point of this book. Our marriage became exciting for us again, after a year or two of drifting apart, not because either Judy or I is naturally a loving or kind person but because we both tried to make what effort we could. And small though that effort was, God was able to use it.

If I intend to start a new store, have prayed and felt God's leading, and see some circumstances shaping up, I will get no further toward my goal by just sitting down to pray some more without doing my part. There comes a time when I've just got to go out and *do it.* We can so easily get lost in spiritual language, in "verbal fog." When we are walking in God's will and according to His principles, there is room for us to move freely and in a certain sense master our circumstances. We can't forget that God is the foundation for it all. But once that foundation is laid, He expects us to diligently and responsibly effect our circumstances by following His commands.

It is a principle that a "faith picture," a vision, becomes reality once we act upon it. This is true in many areas. Daily I witness God bringing into reality the vision He has given me for our store. It hasn't come about automatically. He gave me the vision and supplied me with the essential ingredients for carrying out that vision. But then He expected me to go to work, to accomplish what He gave me to do. Every worthwhile thing comes about because someone has worked hard to bring a faith picture into reality.

This is something I am anxious to teach Patrick and Robin—how to bring their faith pictures to life. One day I will sit down with them and ask, "What shall we make Mommy for Christmas?"

And they'll probably blurt out all kinds of hasty answers. "A toy, a box, a chair, a picture . . . !"

And that's good. Creativity will already have begun in them the moment they have seen something in their minds.

Then we'll narrow it down to one thing, perhaps a little wooden box for some of Judy's sewing things. Then I will ask them to draw a picture of it. With a little help and with some modifications here and there, we will probably be able to come up with something that looks substantially like what we want to make.

Once we have a picture, we will go down to the shop and get to work. We will tackle the project one thing at a time. And before long something which was once just an idea in our heads will be taking shape before us.

And I'm going to explain to them about faith and making one's faith alive and real by belief and acting upon that belief. I want them to know that if they diligently pursue any godly goal, and are willing to make the effort and pay the price to reach that goal, they will. It applies to making a box, starting a store, evangelizing a city, or establishing communication and love in your home.

Well, the point is this. Don't let this book be just religious words to you. If you want it to work, you've got to do it. And please realize that we are a "Christian family in action" merely because we are struggling *daily* to apply the principles too. The Christian life can never be put on "automatic." We *make it work* every day, every moment, doing the very things we have discussed here.

Just today I became frustrated at the store. We were terribly busy and I had a couple of things to do which just couldn't wait. I found myself being "short" with customers as I tried to hurry back to my desk. I was deliberately trying to ignore the very people God has given me to serve. I had no business being upset. But I gave in to my human weakness. That does not excuse me, though. God's power is there for me whenever I need it and choose to let it operate.

Last week Judy, in tears, called me at the store. Robin was apparently getting two of his molars and must have been in terrific pain. He had cried most of the day, writhing around on the floor, sobbing and sobbing. Patrick, too, didn't feel well. So they were both crying and upset and demanding her total attention.

She called me and pleaded with me for an answer. "What can I do?"

But I was silent on the phone. I just didn't have a

ready answer. I had *no* answer. It was a hard day. Being a Christian family does not assure ready and easy answers.

I am sometimes tempted to think I am out of step as a Christian because of all the trials I seem to face. I occasionally hear an exuberant testimony and wonder, "Why don't I feel like that?"

Then I realize, "No Christian feels like that all the time. Not even the person with that glowing testimony."

God does give us high spots for certain purposes. But life isn't lived on emotions. Over the long haul, over a lifetime, we must rigidly stick to the principles God has given us in the Bible and live by them. We can't expect God to keep our motivation high by feelings or emotions. That is why I chose not to try to "fire you up" with an exciting ending. I wouldn't want to send you on your way with a false motivation. There is simply no substitute for responsibly and diligently *doing it*.

And to me that is exciting. God has given me certain responsibilities and gifts and has clearly laid down the principles I must conform to in order to make the most of them. I can confidently face situations knowing that God is over it all. He has given me the capacity to deal with anything He sends my way.

This does not make it easy. To increase our strength and to keep us always depending on Him and His principles, God does send things into our lives that are tough. I know our family will encounter much bumpy water ahead. We may have some real problems with one or more of our children. There will continue to be a host of perplexing questions to face. But that's okay because God's purpose is behind it. The problems won't be easy to solve. But if we persevere in holding diligently to living according to God's commands, they will be overcome.

APPENDIX 1

Nursing

The fact that natural, God-given breast milk is nutritionally superior to anything else that a baby can be given is almost universally accepted. And not only did Judy want to nurse from a purely physical and nutritional standpoint, she also saw the need of a newborn child to feel the warmth, security, and love of his mother through nursing. God certainly designed the female body and the instinctive sucking of infants to go together.

However, another factor, certainly nonexistent in other times and cultures, was to cause us many frustrations. That was societal pressure. For some reason nursing today seems to be nearly as controversial a subject in some circles as discipline or politics. Everyone has a view, and usually these views are held with a passion. If a woman intends to involve herself in a discussion on nursing, she had better prepare herself for a battle.

First there are the growing and enthusiastic ranks, which include organizations like La Leche League, for whom nursing has opened new vistas of joy in relating to their young children. Quotes from eager breastfeeding mothers are so numerous it is impossible to narrow it down to just a few:

In my opinion breastfeeding is one of the most precious gifts God has given to women.[1]

The newborn baby has only three demands. They are

> warmth in the arms of its mother, food from her breast, and security in the knowledge of her presence. Breast-feeding satisfies all three.[2]

Then on the other side are those mothers who either do not want to nurse or are unable to and who use bottles and formula instead.

At first it would seem that two different ways of nourishing a newborn child would be logical. After all, every situation is different. To try to apply one simple formula to every mother and every baby is as silly as saying that every disciplinary problem raised by a three-year-old toddler can successfully be handled in exactly the same manner. This is obviously untrue. But when it comes to nursing, women on both sides of the issue seem to adamantly suggest that "*this* is the way it is!"

I like the title of a book we carry in our store by Eugenia Price—*No Pat Answers.* Now, that is a brilliant title. Life can be largely summed up in that phrase—there just aren't any easy answers. And that, I think, is the difficulty encountered by many new mothers, and it was faced by Judy also. The nursing advocates flood their literature with one pat answer after another, all summed up by, "*Everyone* can nurse—everyone can and everyone should!"

Schedules are given, advice is offered as if every woman's physical makeup and emotional outlook are identical. "If you don't have enough milk, just do such and such and *it will increase.*" "When weaning, do this, and this, and this and this will naturally follow." Pat answers! What about the woman who follows the directions exactly but does not achieve the prescribed results? No allowance is given for her case.

Women advocating bottle feeding are usually no better. Their answers are often pat too, though different. Their opposition to breastfeeding, often merely a defense mechanism against insensitive pressure, seems often to ignore many of the natural and wonderful things about it.

The results of this division is frustration for many new mothers. A very close friend tried to nurse for a few days after the birth of her first child but had no immediate success (due largely to the pressure of relatives and her limited knowledge of some of the obstacles encountered even in successful nursing). But afterwards, rather than receiving the help and counsel she needed from others who had gone on before her, she was unknowingly condemned for her lack of success. Insensitive pressure can stifle motivation quicker than anything.

This attitude is classically demonstrated in many current books:

> All successful nursing mothers unite in regarding the bottle feeding mother with pity—the same pity a happily married woman feels for a frigid wife. She just doesn't know what she's missing.[3]

> This impoverishment [from not nursing] will affect her whole general well-being ... nonbreastfeeding [is] deprivation of the baby ... nonbreastfeeding [is] a danger to society.[4]

It is easy to see why many women approach the whole subject of nursing with a guilt complex associated with possible failure. Anyone who listened to such words would quite naturally feel guilty if all didn't go just right. How could such a mother help but feel she was failing as a mother to her child when she changed over to a bottle? If his whole life is going to be hindered as a result, what is the unsuspecting mother to think?

Fortunately there *are* two sides to this question, as with most. From our experiences (I should say, from Judy's), we developed a strong desire to share with women on both sides of the fence this simple advice, "God is certainly big enough to work no matter where you find yourself. Don't let pressure of any kind rob you of the joy that either bottle feeding *or* breastfeeding can bring."

Appendix 2

Further Excellent Reading

In my thinking and growing over the years I have been given enormous guidance by the writings of various authors. They have helped me through some shaky times when my mind seemed nothing but questions, and they have helped to solidify my thinking in many areas since.

I have, therefore, an almost instinctive desire to share their message and their books. I imagine this is clear from much of what I have said earlier. But I want now to emphasize again that many of the principles I have laid down are not original to me. I am endebted to men like Christenson and Dobson in more ways than I probably even realize. Without their writings there may have been no story for me to tell.

So I want to give you a brief introduction to some of the authors and books which have been significant in my growth. I want this to be more than a recommended reading list. I have before me at this moment nearly thirty books dealing with the family, which I would recommend as helpful. But rather than simply listing these, I want to concentrate on the key books, the ones I would consider essential.

If you really want to understand God's dealings in the family structure, I would say these books are foundational and necessary. These books are not optional. They are musts.

The Christian Family by Larry Christenson. This is the standard work on the family from a biblical standpoint. All aspects are discussed and authority is presented as the guiding principle, which forms the basis for all family relationships. If you could buy just one book, make it this one. It is excellent.

Dare to Discipline by James Dobson. The first of Dobson's books deals with the principle of consistent discipline and how to effectively carry it out.

Hide or Seek by James Dobson. In his second book Dobson goes beyond simple discipline into the building of self-esteem and confidence into children by our behavior toward them.

The Total Woman by Marabel Morgan. A book for women on how to "put romance back into your marriage" by loving and submitting to your husband. Though maybe not the "total answer," the value of its message can be measured by the number of marriages it has excitingly turned around.

What Wives Wish Their Husbands Knew About Women by James Dobson. A very helpful book for husbands who want better to understand their wives. Deals with moods and pressures women face and how husbands can help.

Jesus Wants You Well by C. S. Lovett. The book which gave us enormous help and insight into achieving a balanced picture of God's principles of health and healing.

Additional highly recommended titles:

Help! I'm a Parent by Clyde Narramore
The Fulfilled Woman by Lou Beardsley
Forever My Love by Margaret Hardisty
Letters to Karen by Charlie Shedd
Letters to Philip by Charlie Shedd
Spiritual Authority by Watchman Nee

Footnotes

Chapter 1

1. Reprinted by permission from *The Christian Family* by Larry Christenson. Published and copyright 1970, Bethany Fellowship, Inc., Minneapolis, Minn., pp. 127, 138.

2. Ibid., p. 40.

3. *Christian Living in the Home* by Jay Adams. Baker Book House, Grand Rapids, Mich., p. 89.

4. Ibid., p. 96.

5. Op. cit. *The Christian Family*, pp. 61-62.

6. Taken from *What Wives Wish Their Husbands Knew About Women* by Dr. James Dobson. Copyright 1975 by Tyndale House Publishers. Used by permission.

Chapter 3

1. Taken from *Hidden Art* by Edith Schaeffer. Copyright 1971 by Edith Schaeffer. Used by permission of Tyndale House Publishers, p. 29.

2. Taken from *True Spirituality* by Francis A. Schaeffer. Copyright 1971 by Tyndale House Publishers, Wheaton, Ill. Used by permission, pp. 9, 13.

3. *The Total Woman* by Marabel Morgan. Fleming H. Revell Co., Old Tappan, p. 27.

Chapter 4

1. *Hind's Feet on High Places* by Hannah Hurnard. Church's Ministry to the Jews, London, England, p. 72.

2. Taken from *Dare to Discipline* by Dr. James Dobson. Copyright 1970 by Tyndale House Publishers, Wheaton, Ill. Used by permission, p. 20.

3. Op. cit. *The Christian Family*, pp. 100, 103.

4. *Between Parent and Child* by Dr. Haim G. Ginott. The Macmillan

Co., New York, N.Y. Copyright 1965 by Dr. Haim G. Ginott, p. 107.

5. Op. cit. *Dare to Discipline*, p. 50.

6. From *Help! I'm a Parent* by Bruce Narramore. Copyright 1972 by the Zondervan Corporation. Used by Permission, p. 106.

7. Op. cit. *Dare to Discipline*, pp. 108-110.

Chapter 5

1. Op. cit. *Dare to Discipline*, p. 125.

2. *Preparing for Parenthood* by Dr. Lee Salk. Copyright 1974 by Dr. Lee Salk, published by the David McKay Co., Inc., New York, N.Y., pp. 174-175.

3. Op. cit. *Dare to Discipline*, p. 56.

4. Op. cit. *The Christian Family*, p. 78.

5. Op. cit. *Dare to Discipline*, p. 29.

6. From *You the Parent* by Larry Richards. Copyright 1974, Moody Press, Moody Bible Institute of Chicago. Used by Permission, p. 41.

7. *Hide or Seek* by Dr. James Dobson. Fleming H. Revell Co., Old Tappan, N.J., p. 82.

8. Ann Landers.

Chapter 6

1. *Jesus Wants You Well* by C. S. Lovett. Personal Christianity, Baldwin Park, California.

Chapter 7

1. *The Return of the King* by J.R.R. Tolkien. Houghton, Mifflin Co., New York, N.Y., p. 239.

Chapter 9

1. Op. cit. *You the Parent*, p. 41.

2. From *Baby and Child Care* by Dr. Benjamin Spock. Simon and Schuster, Inc., New York, N.Y. Used by permission, p. 473.

3. Ibid., p. 203, 111.

Chapter 10

1. Op. cit. *What Wives Wish Their Husbands Knew About Women*, pp. 45, 47.

2. Op. cit. *Hide or Seek*, pp. 53-55.

3. Op. cit. *The Total Woman*, p. 36.

4. Ibid., p. 65.

5. Ibid., p. 96.

Chapter 11

1. Op. cit. *Dare to Discipline*, pp. 37-38.
2. Ibid., pp. 39-40.
3. Ibid., p. 55.
4. Op. cit. *Christian Living in the Home*, p. 120.
5. From *A Parent's Guide to the Emotional Needs of Children* by Dr. David Goodman. Hawthorn Books, Inc., New York, N.Y., pp. 81-82.

Chapter 12

1. From *Twins and Supertwins* by Amram Scheinfeld. J. B. Lippincott Co., p. 72.

Chapter 13

1. Op. cit. *Twins and Supertwins*, p. 89.
2. Op. cit. *Hide or Seek*, p. 104.
3. Op. cit. *Dare to Discipline*, pp. 59, 77.

Appendix 1

1. From *The Joy of Being a Woman* by Ingrid Trobisch. Harper and Row Publishers, New York, N.Y. Used by Permission, p. 100.
2. From *Childbirth Without Fear* by Dr. Grantly Dick-Read. Harper and Row Publishers, New York, N.Y.
3. From *Nursing Your Baby* by Karen Pryor. Harper and Row Publishers, New York, N.Y., p. 4. Used by permission.
4. Op. cit. *Joy of Being a Woman*, pp. 100-105.